My Way Around

Journeying the Infinite Spiral of Life

My Way Around – Journeying the Infinite Spiral of Life

By Wendy Ann Zellea

©2019 Happy Awareness Publications

Printed in the United States of America.
ISBN: *978-1-7321775-2-9*

My Way Around

Journeying the Infinite Spiral of Life

WENDY ANN ZELLEA

Happy Awareness Publications, LLC.
Maywood, New Jersey

This book is dedicated to my Mother, Selma Grace Baratta, 1926-2009, and my Father, Martin William Zellea, 1922-2008, without whom there would be no story.

I wish to give thanks to James Tyberonn for supporting me as an author and encouraging me to write this book ... and to my Soul Family for their continued support.

In memory of Bev Sutton, 1961- 2019...

CONTENTS

My Way

Round and round, up and down, on the Infinite Spiral of Life. It is said that life is a circle, but I feel it is more like a spiral, always moving higher, or in some cases, lower. On each turn of the spiral, it is possible to look back, or forward, to see where one has been or where one is bound. The spiral may seem slippery during challenging times. One may feel as though they are sliding back down to where they have already been. Other times it may appear as though they are being transported up many turns of the spiral, rapidly and effortlessly, with assistance of an unseen force.

One may see other lifetimes on the spiral, above, alongside, or below. During auspicious times, the veil that separates these incarnations may become very thin, allowing memories of simultaneous lives or prophetic visions of what may lie ahead. These visions are possible as one connects with other lifetimes in which similar events may be happening. It is helpful to remember that in this current life, bound by rational, logical, deductive thinking, humans are primarily limited to the types of experiences only available in the Third Dimension. Once one embraces the quantum or spiritual view of things, which is not bound by matter, they become aware of an expanded reality. Then mystical things can happen.

My story, in more practical terms, is one of guidance, allowance, and the rewards of living life as an adventure. When I look back, I know that some of the choices I made in the past are not choices I would make now. Even so, I do not wish to lessen the value of any part of my life, because of what I did in the past. Perhaps my experiences may seem difficult for some to grasp, but they are all real and true, from a certain point of view, for truth is what one chooses to believe. Throughout all that has happened, I proceeded with a belief that things would turn out well and, in retrospect, they did.

My story is not just one of an unusual life; it is also one of personal and spiritual growth. I have done many things and been many places, but what stands out for me, as my greatest accomplishment, is the journey I made to find my place in the world, and the discovery that there is still much out there to be learned. Yet, I have a feeling that what I wish to discover is not really new, just forgotten.

I live on the same street where I was born. Others may also be able to say the same thing, but my journey took me away, and then brought me back to where I began, so that I could begin again. Currently, I work in the IT department of a major corporation and I also write esoteric books. It creates a good balance and keeps me grounded, but not too grounded. I love technology and I love spirituality. I love my life. I have always been adaptable, a trait that I consider essential to survival.

My childhood was a happy one, for I had a loving family. Even though I grew up very close to New York City, in the New Jersey suburbs, my world was very small. Movies, books, and music were my pastimes. Hours were spent watching TV, the wonderful shows of the 1950's.

My parents were forward thinking intellectuals, with an extremely high standard of moral values. I was instilled with almost no religious training, which was an asset for me in my spiritual journey, for I did not have to overcome traditional religious indoctrination, as others might have.

My teenage years were in the 1960's. Things were rapidly changing. Young people were abandoning cultural beliefs and creating new ones. As a result of embracing this new freedom, I can safely say that I spent most of my adult life on the fringes of society. At times, it was difficult, because when one is young, they want to fit in, but looking back, it was a blessing.

Bienvenidos a Mexico

I will begin my tale in the middle, and explain how I came to be an author, Literary Channel, and Luminary. The year was 1985. It was a rainy, chilly Christmas Eve in San Cristóbal de las Casas, in Chiapas, Mexico. I sat in the central plaza, watching the young Mayan girls and their mothers, selling crafts to the many tourists that were walking about in the gloomy weather. The smell of pine trees and corn tortillas filled the damp air. As I sat and watched the world go by, I thought to myself, here I am sitting all alone at Christmas, not knowing what to do with my life. I am in my mid-thirties and have nothing to show for it.

Now, the part about not having anything to show for my life was not true. I had accomplished quite a bit of personal development, but that day I was just feeling a bit sorry for myself. I never wanted to follow the crowd, or live entrenched in the fog of the collective consciousness. I had stepped off the cliff of conformity and had not fallen.

As I sat in the annoying drizzle, I began to think about the rest of my life, well perhaps not my entire life, actually just the immediate future. I know what I don't want, but not what I want. Just then, a cute guy walked by. Well, maybe things are not so bad after all, I surmised when I saw him. We exchanged glances and he came walking towards me.

"Hello, where are you from?" he began, in the usual friendly way that young tourists tend to greet one another when traveling in such areas.

I was glad to have someone to talk to. He seemed nice enough and he spoke English. I speak Spanish quite well, I must say, but I longed for a conversation in English after a week in Mexico.

"I'm from New Jersey, how about you?" I replied.

He explained that he was from Ohio but was attending graduate school in Boston. He had a few weeks off and then would be going back.

"Where are you headed from here?" I inquired.

"Oh, I'm going to Belize tomorrow," he said.

"Where's Belize?" I asked.

"It's the country that borders this one. It is about fifty miles from here. You mean you haven't heard of it?" he replied.

Borders this one, I must appear quite ignorant. How could I never have heard of Belize when I have been to Mexico at least four times?

"No, I haven't," I said.

"Where are you going next?" he asked.

"I'm not sure. I really have no plans, actually for the rest of my life."

We chatted for a few more minutes, and then he went on his way. That night, as I sat in the courtyard of my hotel, drinking a cup of tea, the same young man walked in.

"Hi there, I see you are staying here too," he said, as he walked over to my table. "May I sit with you? A hot cup of tea would certainly take off the chill of the evening?"

"I don't mind, have a seat," I replied.

I asked him what it was like in Belize and he proceeded to tell me a little about his last trip there.

"It sounds lovely, maybe I will go there when I leave San Cristóbal," I said.

"If you like, we could travel to Belize together," he suggested. "It is a beautiful place. I am going to Caye Caulker, an island off the coast."

Even though I had just met this young man, it sounded like a marvelous idea. It felt right. I was tired of traveling alone and having to deal with local men flirting with me at every turn of the bend. It would be a relief to travel with a man for a while. I felt that this young person appeared at a time when I needed guidance and inspiration. He was pointing me in a direction in which it seemed I was meant to go. I had no idea how important Belize would be, both in my life and my spiritual journey. As always, I was being watched over.

The next morning, we left. We decided to take the scenic route through Guatemala and spend a few days in Antigua and Lake Atitlán. The bus rides were long, but we did not mind. The mountain scenery was beautiful, and we had plenty of time to talk. Barry told me that he had been there, with his girlfriend, a couple of years earlier. Afterwards she dumped him for his best friend. Now he was visiting all the places they had been together. He seemed lonely. I felt like he was also happy to be travelling with someone.

"What about you?" he asked, after telling me his tragic story, "what are you doing down here? You looked very intense when I first saw you in the zócalo."

"I like San Cristobál, the climate and the culture. I am at a turning point in my life and I thought a trip might help me decide what comes next. I just ended a thirteen-year relationship. I guess I am also visiting places we went together, but perhaps not for the same reason as you. I've done many things in my life, but I do not wish to go back to any of them."

"What was his name?" he asked.

"His name was Jim. We met when I was in graduate school in Norman, Oklahoma. He was a high school math teacher but dropped out. He was a bit of a hippie and did not want to pursue a straight life. More than anything else, I think he wanted to shock his conservative parents.

I was naive then. I had no idea what the world was like, outside of the academic environment in which I had been living. He swept me off my feet, and we fell in love. I was twenty-two years old and he was twenty-four. He filled my head with new ideas and I embraced them. We were very close for thirteen years, but now it is over."

I was not ready to talk about it in any more detail, especially with someone I had just met. As the bus bounced along, I looked out the window at the small houses that dotted the side of the road, most of which looked very poor. I wondered about the people living in them, what kind of life they had, and if they were happy.

We stayed in beautiful Lake Atitlán, Guatemala for two days, then travelled to Puerto Barrios, a small town on the tiny bit of Caribbean coast belonging to Guatemala. From there, we caught a ferry to Belize. We were both eager to reach Caye Caulker, which Barry assured me would be the highlight of the trip. The bus ride to Belize City was long, about eight hours, over an unpaved, dusty road. When we arrived, it was too late to get a boat to the island, so we stayed the night. It was hardly a city, but a big port town, filled with run-down buildings and open drains. The harbor was quite picturesque though, with white, wooden sailboats bobbing up and down in the dirty water.

In the morning, we had a delicious breakfast of eggs and Fry Jack, a flour tortilla fried in coconut oil. Afterwards, we headed to the Marine Terminal, to catch a boat to Caye Caulker. In 1985, all the boats going to Belize City left the Caye at 6am. Then they all returned to the island at about noon. It was a ridiculous system that left tourists stranded overnight in the city, if they arrived later in the day, which most did. Over the years, as tourism increased, the boat captains figured out that staggering the arrival and departure times would not cut into their profits, rather it would increase them.

As we pulled out of the harbor, I felt the warm Caribbean breeze against my face. It felt good, after the heat of Belize City. The boat ride to the island, in a large skiff, takes about forty-five minutes. The first fifteen minutes were not promising, as the water was still rather murky. Then we passed through some mangroves and emerged into a clear turquoise sea. The further we went, the clearer and bluer the water became, until I could see the shadow of the clouds on the sea floor, through the shallow water below.

The second largest barrier reef in the world runs along the coast of Belize. I fell in love instantly with the distant view of the turquoise water, the white line of the waves breaking over the corals, and the sapphire blue of the deeper water beyond the reef. It was already becoming worth the long trip I had just made.

In 1961, Caye Caulker had been split in two by Hurricane Hattie, resulting in a channel between the two halves of the island. The channel, called The Split, created a convenient shortcut for boats to go to the back of the island. The channel was also a great place to swim. The southern half of the island, which was approximately one mile long and three short blocks wide, was the inhabited portion. The northern part of the island remained unpopulated for a time.

The economy of Caye Caulker was primarily lobster fishing and tourism. Tourists came to experience the Caribbean, snorkel, and scuba dive. The locals spoke Creole, a colloquial form of English, heard throughout the Caribbean. At first, it was almost impossible for me to understand, but I quickly became used to its rhythm and simplicity. For example, when speaking Creole, if one wishes to ask another person, what's going on, they say, da wadda gowan? It is a singsong way of speaking, which reflects the rhythmic island way of life.

Islanders spent a good part of the day either outside, or inside with unscreened windows left open. The Trade Winds, which came from the East, were usually blowing. To a large extent, the quality of island life depended upon the breeze. When it blew, life was good. When it did not, it was hot, and sand flies and mosquitos made their appearance. On calm days, mosquito coils were burned inside, with windows shut, and coconut husks burned outside.

Ideally, homes were built on the windward side of the island. However, most of the land on that side had already been allocated to the original settlers that had built it up with houses and hotels. After that, homes were built farther towards the back of the small island. To escape from the bugs, houses were generally built on stilts, some up to twelve feet off the ground. This served a double purpose, as laundry could be hung underneath the house.

In addition to the locals, there was a community of expatriates, primarily from the US, Canada, and Europe. Most came only in the winter months. This group could be broken down into two loosely defined sub-groups. One group did not socialize much with the locals and had a bit of an elitist attitude. The other group, primarily women, found themselves in romantic relationships with island men.

Something happens when a person steps off the boat on to a tropical island. They seem to temporarily forget themselves. I am not certain if it is the climate, the scenery, or both. Most island romances, involving tourists, only lasted as long as the vacation. After all, when they returned home, no one knew what went on. The island men work very hard. Most are in extremely good physical shape. Need I say more? The problem is that the cultural divide, between tourists and locals, is very wide and very deep. Women, who found they were falling in love, had a hard road ahead of them.

One evening as I sat on the verandah of my hotel, taking in the early evening breeze, after returning from watching the sunset on the back pier, I was chatting with a woman that was also staying there. In the course of our conversation, she asked me for some advice. She had fallen in love with a young Rastafarian. This nice young man lived in a tree house, in a part of the island where a few of the other Rastas had also built similar structures. She explained to me that she did not know what to do and asked me if I thought there was any future in their relationship.

"Are you sure you want my opinion?" I asked.

"Yes, I do, Wendy, I need someone's opinion. At the moment, I am only guided by passion," she said.

"Jenny, the man lives in a tree," I replied. "What expectations do you have for the two of you? Just have a good time and when your vacation is over, go home. I have seen those tree houses. You cannot stay here and live in his wretched little half-built structure. You also cannot take him home with you. He is a fisherman. He will be a fish out of water up there. I do not see much future for the two of you. Don't get me wrong. I know who he is and I like him, but you must see that I am right."

I believe she did see, for she went home a week later. She came to thank me for my advice before she left. Not long afterwards, the village council trimmed down the branches where the houses were built and the residents moved elsewhere. I believe even the Rastas knew it could not last, but they made their statement. I respected them for wanting to live close to nature, but perhaps just not that close.

Three months after I arrived, my finances were running low. I was preparing to return home to New Jersey. One evening, as I sat in my usual spot on the verandah, which stretched the length of the hotel, I began chatting with a man that had been staying there for about two weeks. I explained that I would be leaving soon, and he asked why.

"Money," I replied, "it is time to go home and find a job."

"That is no reason to leave, if you don't want to. Listen, I just received an extremely large insurance settlement. My business burned down," he explained, winking. "I will lend you some money and you can pay me back, or not."

He kindly lent me a few thousand dollars. I felt it was a confirmation that I was meant to stay on the Caye. So, there I was, after a thirteen-year unhappy relationship, free and living in paradise.

Island Life

I rented a small house, separated from the sea by only a narrow, sandy street. The price was reasonable and the view fantastic. I had no purpose in mind, except to write, relax, and enjoy life. Snorkeling was the main activity for tourists visiting the Caye, but I had not tried it. I was not yet drawn to going to the reef. Then one day all that changed.

Each morning, the tour guides that took people on snorkeling trips, stood in various locations on the sandy street, looking for potential customers. They were usually successful, as most often the tourists were looking for them. One particular morning, I was on my way to one of the small island grocery shops, when I passed by one of the guides.

"Want to go to the reef on my sailboat today, Miss?" he asked.

"I hadn't thought," I replied.

"I've seen you around," he continued. "You done rent Rico's house, no true?"

"Yes, I have been living there for a couple of months," I said.

"Where are you from?" he asked.

"I'm from the States, New Jersey. Listen, I might go sometime, but not today, thanks."

"Well, I hope when you do go, you go with me," he replied, grinning.

After that, when he passed my house, if he caught my eye, as I sat on the verandah or by the window, he smiled and waved. One morning I decided to see what the reef was all about. I walked out onto the street and saw him at his usual spot.

"I've decided I would like to go snorkeling. Are you going out today?"

"I already have three people, with you it is four, so, ya mon, it looks like we de go. Be here at eleven o'clock."

"How much does the trip cost?" I asked.

"For you, I no de charge," he said.

"That is very kind, but I insist on paying."

"Ok then, it's twenty US dollars. We go to two stops on the reef and then another stop at Hol Chan Marine Reserve. Then we go to San Pedro on Ambergris Caye for lunch. You will have to rent your own snorkeling gear," he explained, in a professional tone.

"How much does that cost?" I asked.

"Five US dollars, there is a place right over there, where you can rent some good gear," he said, as he pointed to a small dive shop.

He did not have a particularly handsome face, but he had a sort of charisma that made one feel happy to be around him.

"Sure, it sounds like fun. I will see you at eleven. Oh, by the way, what's your name?" I asked.

"They call me Samosa," he replied.

"After the food?"

"Yes, it is something very delicious," he said, seeming very proud of himself to be named after a yummy food.

I liked his manner; he was not flirty, like many of the other men I had spoken to on the island. "Ok, Samosa, I'll be back at eleven."

"What's your name, Miss?" he asked, as I turned to walk towards the gear rental shop.

"I'm Wendy. I'll see you later, Samosa."

"Ya, mon, lata," he replied, smiling.

After renting a mask, snorkel, and fins, I went to a small grocery shop and bought some juice and snacks. By that time, it was 10:45. I stopped at my house to put on my bathing suit and grab a towel, sunscreen, water, and a few other items. I met the group on the street at eleven o'clock and we all headed out to the end of the bridge, the island name for the pier, where the thirty-four-foot, wooden sailboat was all ready to leave.

Most of the sailboats on the island, works of boat-building art, were constructed by a handful of native islanders. The aging master boat-builders were a dying breed and eventually there would be no more like them, as the younger men were not interested in learning to build boats. Fiberglass boats, which were easier to maintain, would take the place of the old wooden lovelies.

There were five people aboard the boat, plus Samosa and a young man with dreadlocks that was his helper. Both crewmembers wore only bathing suits and had muscular bodies that could only be created by natural hard work. It was a perfect day for sailing, which Samosa informed me, was not unusual for the Cayes. A boom box played Reggae music, as we sailed out towards the reef. When we arrived at the first stop, the other tourists put on their snorkeling gear and began to jump in the water.

"Samosa, I've never been snorkeling. To be honest, I am a bit nervous about it. I think the movie Jaws ruined it for me."

"No mon, you no have to worry 'bout sharks here. Only some of them will bother you. If you see one, you just swim back. Mek we go, I will show you around my world. Do not touch the corals, especially the yellow ones. That is fire coral and it will burn you."

I jumped in the sea and immediately tasted the extremely salty water. Then I dipped my head under the surface. It was truly another world, filled with spectacular coral and dozens of varieties of tropical fish. I was not used to seeing creatures in the wild. It was awe-inspiring. Samosa brought along a homemade Hawaiian Sling spear gun. He swam around as if he was looking for something. Stopping for a moment, he stretched the rubber tubing that held the spear, then let it go, hitting the fish dead center in the head. I watched as he swam down about thirty feet to retrieve his spear and his catch. He swam back to me, holding the fat black snapper above the water with the spear.

"He will be dinner tonight," he said, upon his return.

"Why do you hold the fish above the water?" I asked.

"So I do not attract sharks with the fish blood." He swam back to the boat and gave the fish to his helper. "Come with me," he said, after he had returned to where I was snorkeling.

The saltiness of the water made it easy to float. Samosa took my hand and we swam together, as he pointed out the resident sea creatures, which I otherwise would not have seen. To him it was a world teeming with lobster, fish, conch, and stingrays nestled in the sand. He dove down about twenty feet, and shot two rock lobsters.

Lobster was plentiful in the sea around Caye Caulker. It was the primary source of revenue, before tourism took over. The local fishermen had formed the Fisherman's Cooperative, where, in the designated seasons, they could sell lobster and conch. Those that had lived on the island the longest, had certain areas in the sea, where they alone could place lobster traps. The off-season was spent building the large trapezoid shaped traps, out of strips of wood. Each trap had an opening on one end. The lobster, in search of shade, entered the trap, but once inside, could not get out.

Not long before the lobster season opened, the fishermen set their traps in the sea. On opening day of the season, they harvested their catch and brought back an abundance of lobster. The co-op only bought the tails that weighed over four ounces. The smaller ones were illegal, but the fishermen took them anyway to sell to the restaurants and to eat at home. Over time, the lobster population became depleted, as the smaller ones had not been left to breed. In a few years, as tourism increased, so did the demand for cheap lobster dinners in the restaurants. A price was paid for the greed of the fishermen, as lobster became scarce.

We all returned to the boat and got ready for the next stop.

"If you like you can come to my house later and try some of the fish soup this guy will be starring in tonight," Samosa said to me, as he picked up the snapper he had caught. "Would you like to?"

"Where is your house?" I asked.

"You are in it right now. I live on the sailboat. I'm a pirate."

"Not a real pirate," I replied, in a skeptical tone.

"A real pirate, Miss. If me never de do snorkeling trips, I would be contra banding lobster and conch to Honduras and picking up bales of weed, dropped overboard by smugglers chased by maritime police. I de live da straight life now, since tourism is so profitable."

"Wasn't that dangerous, what about the police?" I asked.

"Maritime can't catch me on the sea," he said proudly. "I know when and where to move. I know the currents and the shoals. I am like a fish in the water. Years ago, before a lot of tourists came, we would spend the entire day diving. There are some divers, right here on the Caye, that can stay under for up to twelve minutes on one breath.

When a free diver goes down to hunt, they first go on a reconnaissance dive to see what is down there. Then once they know where all the sea creatures in the area are hanging out, they dive down again and shoot a bunch, all at once. They will come to the surface with a few fish, some lobster, and some conch, which are the easiest since they do not really move much at all. Then they go back for the rest."

We made one more stop at the Marine Reserve, which has an abundance of fish, Moray eels, sharks, barracuda, and almost every variety of Caribbean sea life. I remained in the boat and basked in the cool breeze in the shade of the jib, while Samosa guided the other tourists. A Mexican family, including the grandmother, came in a long fiberglass skiff and all of them, except the captain, jumped in the water. The captain then poured a bucket of sardines in the water, near the snorkelers, which resulted in a fish feeding frenzy, including sharks. The tourists all took photos with underground cameras. I, still with memories of Jaws, watched from the boat.

We had lunch in San Pedro on Ambergris Caye, about three miles from the Marine Reserve, and then headed back. When we arrived, the others exited the boat, thanking the captain, and saying they enjoyed the trip.

"Thanks," said Samosa, as I handed over $20 US plus a tip. "Will I see you later for fish tea?"

"Fish tea, what is fish tea?" I asked. It sounded awful.

"It is fish soup," he explained. "It will be done in about an hour if you would like to come back aboard and taste a fisherman's cooking. It is the best, you know."

"If it is the best, then I must try it. I will see you later. What do you like to drink?" I asked.

"I drink Belikin Stout," he replied.

I liked him. He seemed like a gentle soul. After a shower and a stop at a bar for four Belikin stouts, the local dark brew, I headed back to the boat. The nearly full moon had risen and shone a beautiful, pale-yellow light that stretched all the way from the reef to the shore, along the sparkling water. I stood at the end of the bridge and called Samosa's name. He came up from below, wearing jeans, a t-shirt, and a bandana, holding his dreadlocks in place. He was tall with broad shoulders, grey eyes, and sun-bleached, dark hair.

We were both thirsty after a day out on the boat and downed one stout each rather quickly. "You ready fa eat now?"

"Yes, I'm ready, the sea made me hungry."

"And now the sea will feed you," said Samosa. "You stay there, I de come right now."

He came back with a bowl of soup and a plate of coconut rice, pulled up a cooler for me to use as a table, and set it all in front of me.

"I know that fish, I met him this afternoon," I said.

"I have thanked him for offering his life so that we can have food. Go through, gal. I de come right now with mines."

I waited until he returned with his food.

"Don't you like it?" he asked, appearing concerned.

"I was waiting for you," I replied.

"No wait 'pon me, gal, eat up," he said, as he began to eat quite robustly. The fish head was in his bowl. "The head is the best part. It's where all the strength of the fish is."

It was the best soup I had ever eaten. "Samosa, this is unbelievable," I said, in between mouthfuls.

"You won't find this food in any restaurant here. This is the real deal. Fresh food, that is the only way you can stay strong in life. People from the States eat too much prepared food. That is why they are weak and sick."

I shook my head in agreement but did not say anything else until I had finished everything. Samosa ate all his food and then chewed the bones until they were a ground meal. Then he spit them in his hand and threw them overboard.

"Want some more?" he asked.

"I would love some more, but there is no room in my belly," I said, feeling very full. "Thank you so much, I won't forget this meal."

"Good, then you will not forget me, since I am the one who cooked it. I de come right now," he said, as he stood up. He took the plates and came back with a deep bowl of water with lime floating in it. "Wash your hands and get the fishy smell off."

We washed our hands, opened the next bottles of stout, and then he lit a joint.

"How long have you lived on a boat?" I asked, as he inhaled deeply and passed the large spliff to me.

"Since I was fourteen," he replied.

"Have you lived in a house since then?" I asked, after I finished choking on the smoke that I tried to inhale. One puff was enough for me. I passed it back to him.

"No, I me get used to the sea. 'Bout how long you will stay here, Wendy?"

"I don't know yet, I might stay for a while. I am starting a new phase of my life; I came here to take time to decide what I will do."

"What kind of work you did in the States?" he asked, as he passed the spliff back to me again.

"No thanks, I'm good. I will stick to the stout. I was a teacher, a musician, and I sold rare phonograph records," but realizing that part would have no meaning in his world, I began over again. "It is like this, some people in the States collect old things that are hard to find. I sold some of these things. Now I am going to try my hand at writing. I have been working on two books for a couple years now and I would like to finish them and get them published."

"You are a smart lady. You are different from most of the tourists I meet and you are very beautiful too."

"Why, thank you," I replied.

"What happened with you and your man, the one you came here with? Did you leave him?" Samosa asked.

"He was not my man; he was only a friend. I met him in Mexico, but he went back to school."

I could have stayed out there in the boat for hours, feeling the cool night breeze and watching the moon, shining on the water, but I thought it was best to go home. "I'll be going now, Samosa. Thanks for everything, it was a great day."

"Mek I walk you back."

"Thank you, that would be nice," I said.

"Do you want to go snorkeling again tomorrow," he asked, as we reached my house.

"No thanks, Samosa, I enjoyed the day, but I am a bit sunburned."

"Good night, Wendy," he said, as he held out his hand. I took his hand, leaned up, and kissed him on the cheek. "Good night and thanks for today."

* * *

A few days later, Mexican vendors came to the island, selling hammocks from the Yucatán peninsula. I bought a beautiful blue and purple one and immediately hung it from the hammock hooks on the verandah. I was in heaven, lying in my new *hamaca*. I felt that my life was back on track. The warm Caribbean breeze blew over me like a gentle kiss. I know why people called this part of the world paradise, I thought, as I dozed off in my new hammock.

* * *

"Good evening," a deep voice said.

I opened my eyes and saw Samosa standing over me. I sat up and he held out his hand, to help me out of the hammock.

"*Me hands dem rough.*" He showed me his hand and I ran my fingers over his skin, which felt like rough leather. "Those are the hands of a fisherman," he said, as he pulled his hand away. He seemed both proud and embarrassed at the same time.

"I really love this house and the view of the sea," I said.

"Maybe you will even stay awhile," said Samosa. "Most people do not stay too long. That is why me one stay single. I don't want to fall for someone who is leaving."

"There must be plenty of good Belizean women here though, aren't there?" I asked.

"Yes, but it's not the same. Once we get to know women from the States or Canada or Europe, we do not want to make a life with Belizean women again. I don't know why, it's just that way with most of the guys who deal with tourists.

When I first started doing reef trips, I went crazy for the women. They threw themselves at me. I knew I was just using them, and they were doing the same, but I did not really care. Then the day came when I fell in love with a woman who was in love with me too but was still going to leave. I knew I would never see her again. After that, I stopped playing with women. I did not want to go through that kind of pain again. I saw what I had been doing in a different light. I found respect for myself realizing what it really means to be a man."

"You meet a lot of women, Samosa, and you are handsome and very nice, you only have to wait for the one that was meant for you."

"I had the one that was meant for me and she left me," he said.

"If she had been meant for you, she would have stayed or found a way for you to be together. I believe she was meant to teach you how to find respect for yourself. Besides, who says there is only one person for each of us? I think there are many people that might be the one. We just stop when one of those ones comes along, that is all. Everything happens as it should, Samosa, sometimes we can never know why, but we should always remember that things happen for the highest good."

"You really think positive, gal."

"Why not, should I sit around and bemoan my fate, when I can create my own positive reality?"

"Perhaps you never have had your heart broken," he said.

"Perhaps I have, but if I continue to think of myself as having been dumped, then I am still being dumped on. I choose to move on. My motto is, I got over it. When you make room in your heart for someone else, someone else will come along. That is why your love had to leave you, so you could find that someone else. Perhaps it was the same for her."

Samosa remained silent for a while and finally said, "Enough talk, let's eat. What did you cook?"

"Cook?" I asked.

"Belizean women cook every day. When the man comes home the food is in the pot on the stove," he explained.

"That is a lovely tradition," I teased, "however, I am not Belizean, and I do not have a man. I am going to take myself out for a lobster dinner to celebrate my new hammock. Didn't you just finish saying that you are not interested in Belizean women?"

"You don't miss a trick, do you, gal. You are not taking yourself out to dinner. I am taking you out so we can both celebrate."

"Oh really, what are you celebrating?" I asked.

"You getting over your broken heart and me thinking about getting over mine," said Samosa.

"Well done," I said, as I offered to shake hands. Instead, he put his arms around me.

"Um, slow down, man, I am not ready to get romantic with anyone. I don't move that fast."

"I am not getting romantic. I only want to see how tall you are, where you come to on me. I want to know if your head comes above my chin."

"And?" I asked, looking up at him.

"Just to…perfect. Let's go, I'm hungry and like Bob Marley says, a hungry man is an angry man."

Getting to Work

I spent my days writing and relaxing. I woke up early and watched the sunrise, as I sat on my verandah with a cup of tea. Each morning there were tourists walking with their backpacks, from their respective hotels to the bridge where the water taxis left for the mainland. More than once, a tourist would stop and ask me where they could get a cup of coffee at that hour. Unfortunately, the one place that had been open early for breakfast, closed when the owner retired.

"Good morning, Rico, are you going to Belize City?" I greeted my landlord as he passed by the house one morning on the way to the boat. I knew he was leaving the island, because he was wearing a shirt and carrying his shoes. The island fisherman almost never wore long pants, except to go to church, and they only put their shoes on right before they stepped off the boat in the city. "Yes, Wendy, I am going to the fisherman's cooperative."

"Excuse me," a woman with a British accent said, as she approached, "do you know where I can get a cup of coffee?"

"No, I'm sorry," I replied.

"You will have to wait until you get to Belize City," Rico added.

"Ok, cheers," she answered, looking disappointed.

"Wendy," Rico said as he turned to me, "why don't you sell coffee in the morning? You could make yourself some money and you would be helping the tourists a lot."

"I guess I could. I mean it is easy enough, since all that is available here is instant Mexican Nescafé. I'll give it a try tomorrow."

That was how my business began. Samosa brought over a piece of plywood and I painted a sign that read: Coffee and Tea 5:30AM. The next morning, I had my first five customers. After that, every day, ten or fifteen people stopped by for a mug of coffee or tea. Many said it was the best coffee they ever had. I wondered how a cup of instant coffee could be that good. I presumed when one is desperate, it probably could.

I was no judge of good coffee, since I preferred tea, but I surmised it must be the rainwater, from the wooden vat in the yard, that made the coffee taste so good. The only safe drinking water on the island came from rainwater, collected as the rain ran off the zinc rooftops. The water then ran into a pipe, connected to a large mahogany or metal vat. Each yard had its own vat and it was understood that one did not get water from someone else's vat without permission.

Most mornings, Samosa came by for coffee and to meet tourists for his snorkeling trips. Occasionally, in the evening, he cooked a delicious meal for both of us, using the fish, lobster, or conch he had caught during the day. He was very particular about how the food was prepared, and he recited every step to me. The garlic and onions had to be chopped very fine and the fish head should always go first into the pot of soup. I wrote it all down with the intention of publishing an authentic Belizean cookbook.

Many of my coffee customers asked me if I also offered breakfast. This led me to give serious thought to what I could include to expand my menu. Beatrice, a Belgian woman that owned a restaurant, had decided to move away to Guatemala. Before she left, she taught me how to make yogurt, from whole powdered milk, the only unsweetened milk available on the island. The final product was delicious, tasting more like sour cream than the non-fat yogurt one finds in the States.

She also gave me the recipe for her homemade granola, consisting of fresh grated coconut, oats, raisins, sesame seeds, and a bit of brown sugar, all toasted in a pan on top of the stove. I added one more touch, a crepe. The final product was fruit crepes with yogurt and granola. It was an instant hit with the tourists, and my restaurant was eventually listed in travel guidebooks. It kept me busy from the time I opened in the morning until noon. The rest of the day was devoted to preparing for the following day, but I still always made time to write.

Everyone on the island thought Samosa and I were a couple. I liked him a lot and he obviously had a huge crush on me, but it was a few months before he finally had the courage to tell me he cared for me. One night, while we were sitting on the verandah, watching the full moon over the water, he turned to me and said, "Wendy."

"Yes, Sam?"

"I love you."

"I know Sam, did you just figure it out?"

"You know? How do you know?"

I did not reply.

"Let me show you what kind of a man I am."

"My dear, I know what kind of a man you are. Just show me how you feel about me."

* * *

Five years later, I was a happy woman. I had a great place to live, a good business, I met people from all over the world, that came to my house each day, and I had a man that loved me. Yes, I loved Sam, but… Whenever there is a but, no more needs to be said. A but only means that he is not always going to be the one. I could not put my finger on it and it did not really matter too much, since everything was so almost perfect.

Technically, Samosa still lived on the boat. He slept at my house until around 4:30am. Then he woke up and went out to the boat to get ready for his day at sea. I slept soundly as he quietly closed the back door. I assumed that he did not want to ruin his image as a pirate by allowing people to see him coming out of a house in the morning. When the island awoke, there he would be, washing down the deck of the sailboat. I did not mind. I preferred having my own space in the morning.

A Dark Cloud

I had been on the Caye for five years. It was December and the island was busy with the Christmas rush of tourists. People were lined up for my delicious, if I say so myself, breakfast, before they went snorkeling or scuba diving. On this particular Friday morning, a balding man with dreadlocks walked in.

"Good morning," he said.

"Good morning," I replied. "Are you here for breakfast?" I felt a chill when I looked at him, and he refused to meet my gaze.

"No, I am looking for Samosa," he said.

"He is getting ready for his snorkeling trip, either on the boat or at the co-op getting gas." I replied.

"Thanks, please tell him Prince was looking for him."

"Sure, no problem," I said, acting busy so I would not have to look at him again.

* * *

"You cook like a Belizean now, Gal, almost as good as I do," Samosa said that evening. He smiled at me, knowing I would tell him that I had surpassed him.

"Oh, by the way, Sam, a guy named Prince was looking for you this morning before you left on your trip. Did he find you?"

"Ya mon, I done talk to him earlier. We went to school together in Belize City. After a while, he went one way and I went another. He is a bit of a hustler now. He gave me some good weed though. He said there is something in it that gives you a real good buzz. They call the joints lovelies."

"What is in it?" I asked.

"I don't know, he didn't really say," he explained, as he ate his rice and beans with stew chicken, "but I smoked it on the boat today. All the guys on the Caye are smoking it."

The good buzz turned out to be crack cocaine. Prince gave it away for free, knowing they would want more. He was the one that could supply them with it.

"That stuff is highly addictive, Sam. You smoke that and you will not be able to stop. You'll be an addict," I said, once I discovered what was going on.

"No gal, you only get hooked on it when you smoke from a pipe, when you freebase, not when you smoke it with the weed."

"Listen Sam, you don't know what you are talking about," I went on, "there are people all over the States hooked on that stuff. It is the most addictive substance around. This is not a joke, man. This is your life. You need to stop smoking that stuff now."

"Don't worry 'bout me, gal," he replied. "I have a strong constitution. I am in control of myself."

"I don't like it. I don't like it at all," I said.

* * *

I did not mention it again, but I knew it was not good. I wondered how it could ever be resolved. There are many faces to substance abuse and many substances that can be abused, including, food, sex, drugs, alcohol, shopping, or any other activity that is done excessively and cannot be controlled. When it came to crack, there were those that smoked the lovelies and remained unaffected. Then there were those who were sprung, or addicted.

The small island was getting a firsthand view of the many faces of addiction. They watched their sons, husbands, neighbors, and nephews fall to the influence of the drug. The worst were the sprung heads, the ones that smoked all the time from a pipe. They spent the entire day doing odd jobs for a little bit of money, so they could go buy another piece of crack. Those that were really hooked, walked around looking in the sand as though they had lost something.

It took only a couple of months after crack was introduced on the island, for the real problem to surface. The crime rate rose on the Caye. The sprung heads would steal anything from anyone, including their own family, to get the drug. Samosa was one of the luckier ones who kept smoking his lovelies and could function normally, for a while at least. Then he began to stay on the boat all night. Other young men from the Caye would join him there to smoke.

I was aware of the change in him and the odd smell that lingered on his clothes. He also began to drink too much. I was glad that he was living on the boat, but I realized I needed to make a clean break.

"Sam," I said one evening, "this isn't working. I cannot be with you if you are going to have crack in your life. I love you, but you are not the same man any more. Please decide what you want, me or crack."

For the first time, I saw a different side of the man I thought I knew. "You can't tell me what to do, I'm a grown man," he began to shout at me, while strutting around in a menacing way. "You women from the States come down here and think you can rule men. Belizean man cannot be ruled. What makes you think I even want you anymore? I will stay away from you, but you better not think you can live in this house with another man. If I see another man living here, I will burn this house down with both of you in it," he said, as he walked out of the door.

Sam did not speak to me after that. I was heartbroken and relieved at the same time. Deep down I knew our relationship was over when he smoked his first lovely. I just hoped he would stop.

Within a week, Samosa was walking around the island with tourist girls. Then I noticed he was with a slim, Swiss girl all the time.

"The gal de smoke crack with him," said Rose, one of my local friends.

"Sorry for her, Rose," I replied.

"He still talks about you, Wendy. He is very jealous of you. He will get crazy if he thinks there is a man here, especially a Belizean man."

"I've had my fill of men right now, Rose. You know how it is when you get out of a relationship. You just want to live in peace, without a man in your life."

"Yes, gal, but you still need a man," she replied.

"I can't think of that right now, Rose. It's not as if we had split up, the man I knew just does not exist anymore. Oh yes, you see him out there walking around with someone else, but he is not the same person."

"For true, gal, he done change," she said in agreement.

In the weeks that followed, I began to realize that I had a slight case of island fever and caught myself thinking of clear, crisp autumn days in New Jersey. It hardly bothered me when I saw Sam and Lisa walking around hand in hand. Then one day I looked out the window and saw that Lisa had a black eye. Over the weeks, Lisa had a few more black eyes. Then she left the island and Sam started coming to my house every few days to talk to me. He knew there was no chance, but he was going to mark his territory. I decided it was time for me to leave, so I made flight reservations, packed up my things, and stored them at Rose's house.

"I will either be back in a couple of months or not, Rico. My belongings are secure, but I don't want to lose this house," I said, as I handed him the rent for two months. "I'll let you know. Thanks for everything."

"I think you are doing the right thing, Wendy. Samosa can be a good man, but he also has a temper, a bad one. You see that woman that just left him. Do you see what he did to her? Better, you leave here for a while. She will be back, then you can return, and he won't bother you."

"Why do you think she would come back, Rico?"

"Oh, she is coming back, all right. She only went home to get more money. Her family is supposed to be rich. He will be good to her until the money runs out and then she will get beaten again."

"You are right, Rico, it is better if I go. I don't really want to see all that. This place is much too small. Please tell your wife thanks for everything."

"I will, Wendy, but where are you going?"

"I am going to Dallas, Texas. I have a friend there I want to visit and I also have some unfinished business, regarding my partner who passed away. I had better go now; the boat will be leaving soon. Do you know where I can get a cup of coffee?" I joked.

"Not anymore, Wendy," he replied, smiling, as if he knew that he would not see me for a long time.

As the plane took off, I felt myself going up the infinite spiral of life once again.

Things I Know Now

My life has been a spiritual journey, yet I have never been more aware of it as in the past fifteen years. I have learned much and gone through extensive personal growth. In the process, I have discovered that a person creates experiences so that they may learn lessons.

So then, why would someone resort to using a drug? Perhaps there is a part of them that they have been hiding, both to themselves and the world. They do this for a time, but eventually they can hide no longer. Along comes a substance that resonates with the secret hidden part of them. When they begin to use the drug, the hidden part emerges and they change. Of course, it might be healthier to go through a process of personal growth, but not everyone has the intention or the will to do so.

I also wondered why I picked a man such as Sam. Oh, I could convince myself that he was so nice, and I never knew about his ugly side, but I do not believe that was the case. No, deep down I knew. Remember the but? I just did not want to see it. I kept it hidden. When it finally emerged, I was forced to create boundaries and stick to them.

In a way, until I got away from him, I was also abusing the same substance as he was. I was not ingesting it physically, but I was getting a daily dose in my Energy Body from being around him. It is not always easy to leave someone you think you love, but in the end, when you see the real person, you find that you only loved the image of them that you had created, not who they truly were. I took that lesson with me into my next relationship.

I have also asked myself, why I was drawn to Belize. Spoiler Alert, in total, I spent fifteen years of my life there. Let me begin by saying that I view the years since 2000, as the consciously focused, spiritual part of my life. I have become aware of many things that most people do not even consider, but that I hold to be true. Again, truth is what one chooses to believe.

Years after I left Belize, I read a book containing Edgar Cayce's readings on Atlantis. He states that parts of Atlantis were in what are now Belize and the Yucatán. Upon reading that, I received the understanding that part of the reason I was there, was because of unresolved issues I had from simultaneously existing lifetimes in Atlantis. My experiences in Belize were an opportunity to overcome personal shortcomings that I had not been able to, in my Atlantean and Mayan incarnations.

In addition, I was integrating ancient codes, brought here eons ago by Star Beings. These codes have since remained embedded in the energetic signatures of particular places on Earth, where ancient beings once flourished. Over time, as a result of living in modern society, the codes that were originally in the default human energy body have been damaged or lost. This explains the desire of many spiritual seekers to visit such places. It was necessary for me to re-integrate the codes as part of my personal Ascension Process. When I think back on all that I have experienced, even when things seemed dark, I know it was all part of a wonderful journey, which is my life.

Big D

Fran, an old college friend from the University of Oklahoma, kindly and graciously invited me to stay with her for as long as I wanted. She was a trust fund baby and had a big house in a lovely old section of Dallas, Texas. I think she wanted the company, as much as helping me out while I sold my collection of rare phonograph records that Jim and I had collected over the years.

Fran knew Jim had died on our last trip to Mexico, but she did not know all the details. She was kind enough not to ask for more than I was ready to offer. Her ex-boyfriend and Jim had been in the same fraternity at the University of Oklahoma, so she knew what he was like before I met him.

"I'm really sorry about Jimmy," she said one evening. "I know it is hard for you to talk about, but if you ever wish to, I will listen."

"Thanks Fran, I might take you up on that when I am ready. What was he like when you knew him in college?"

"He was really smart, smarter than most of his fraternity brothers, but he was troubled," she said. "Of course, you know he was adopted."

"Yes, he spoke of it often," I replied. "I believe it was part of his problem, or at least he made it so. I could not know what it must be like to be adopted, so I tried not to judge him harshly for wearing it as a badge. When he was twenty-one, he decided he wanted to know his real parents."

"Yes, he was raised by a couple on a farm in Oklahoma City," Fran added.

"His adopted father was deaf and owned a dog kennel," I continued. "His adopted mother was, well, not the warmest person. I believe he grew up desperate for love. He finally found his birth mother, living right there in Oklahoma City. She met his biological father while he was stationed there, during the war. They married and she became pregnant with Jim. While on leave, his father went back to Massachusetts to tell the family about the marriage, but they were against it because she was not Jewish. Her family was against him because he was Jewish, convincing her to put the baby up for adoption.

He eventually met his biological father. I went with him to Cape Cod to visit him. The resemblance was uncanny; they both had black eyebrows and blondish hair. They also had the same birthday. Their personalities were very similar too, outgoing, funny, and smart.

His father, who died of a heart attack two years after I met him, had remarried and had two children. Then two years later, the daughter died in a boating accident. Two years after that, the son died in a car wreck. I lost my baby boy, his son, at birth, and five years later, Jim died."

"He also got a high school girl pregnant when we were in college, the baby was stillborn," Fran added.

"Golly", we both said simultaneously, and then remained silent for quite some time.

"Poor Jimmy, he was never really happy," said Fran, after a minute or two.

"Actually, he seemed happy when I first met him," I replied, "but I think it was because he was around me. I have always been a happy person. I believe that is why I attract unhappy men. They think I can make them happy too, but that isn't the way it works, is it?"

"Wendy," said Fran, after we had lunch one day, "I can help you bring some of the records over here when you are ready. I think it would be fun. I have a cart in the garage we can use."

"Sure, that would be great. How about tomorrow? I might as well get started on sorting and pricing them. I have been here for a month already and I don't want to overstay my welcome."

"I've already told you, Wendy, I am glad you are here. I get bored in this big house all by myself; I am enjoying having a visitor. By the way, how will you sell them?" she asked.

"After I get them sorted and ready, I am going to call some record collector/dealers that I know.

That is probably all it will take. I have some very rare 45s with picture covers. I actually paid $2000 for one Elvis double EP."

"How did you and Jim manage to acquire all these records anyway?" Fran asked.

"We travelled around the country and went to second hand stores, flea markets, juke box vending companies, and radio stations. When we first started, it was easy, because records were plentiful. There are only a finite amount of records though, especially now that people buy cassette tapes. We went to record conventions, where we traded up the ones we did not want, for the more valuable ones we did want. We only collected a record if we liked the music on it. It was fun at first, but to be honest, I became rather bored with it after a while."

The next morning was a bright and sunny April day. I took Fran out for breakfast and then we drove to the storage facility. When I opened the door to the climate-controlled unit, a wave of emotion blew over me, as I viewed the boxes of LPs and 45s that Jim and I had collected over the years. In a way, I was sorry that I was going to sell them, but in another way, I was glad. As I looked through all the beautiful, rare picture sleeves that covered each disk, I remembered where we had acquired each one. Fran admired the Elvis and Beatles imported EPs, with picture covers, and the rare 50's R&B promo 45s on colored vinyl.

I thought of the last night Jim and I were together, driving through Mexico. It was July, near Oaxaca, it was late, and we were tired....

"Look at this one," Fran said, as she pulled out a Marilyn Monroe 78, with a picture of Marilyn on the label.

"Oh yes," I replied, "That is a promo of River of No Return. Nice one, isn't it?"

It took the rest of the day, but finally all the records, in their little cardboard carrying cases, were loaded in the car, brought back to Fran's house, and sitting in my room. A month later, I had sold the entire collection to a record dealer I knew, trusted, and liked. We were both happy with   the   deal   we   made.

What Now?

Now that my affairs were in order, I had to think about what to do next. Yes, I could be a full-time writer, but I had to find my own place to live. I was missing the Caye, but I would not go back if Sam were there. Even if I did go back, I would not want to run a restaurant again. It was too much work.

There was no refrigerator in the little house I rented, which was not unusual, as most people on the island used ice coolers. Shaved ice was available at the Fisherman's Co-op for one Belize dollar, fifty cents US, for a five-gallon bucket. Buckets were plentiful, arriving either full of pigtail or lard, both popular food items. When the contents were sold, the store washed the buckets and sold them for two dollars each. A bucket full of ice weighed about twenty pounds. Many mornings I carried that weight, four blocks from the Co-op to my house. Ideally, I could find a young lad to get the ice for me, but that was rare. Needless to say, I became very strong.

Washing clothes by hand was another upper body exercise, but I rather enjoyed the process. There were no washing machines or laundromats on the island. Instead, people washed their clothes outside, by hand. There was a long, stone rectangular slab in my yard, which was used for scrubbing. It stood about waist high, and had a shallow sink in the middle. A zinc roof covered the area and a faucet provided water. Pigtail buckets were used for soaking and rinsing. After ringing the clothes, they were hung out to dry. When taken off the line in the evening, after the sun no longer shone upon them, they were as soft as if they had been in a dryer. All things considered, outside on a warm Caribbean day, in the shade, with my hands in the water and the breeze blowing, it was a fairly tolerable task.

One day, as I was doing my washing, and hanging the clothes out on the line, my neighbor, a ninety-three-year-old woman, was sitting on her verandah. She called me over and said, "You have to turn the pants inside out or they will not dry evenly." Not wanting to offend her, I followed her instructions. It turned out she was right.

Occasionally after that, when she was outside catching the breeze, she would call me over to talk. One day she began to tell me, "I don't want no more man. My son de look for one man for me, but me no want no more man."

Then she went on to say that she had been a fisherwoman and that she had helped form the fisherman's cooperative. "I me go fishing, come home, clean my fish, sell them to the co-op, and cook dinner, before my husband even came from fishing."

She had also been the island midwife. When I told her that I had lost a baby because it was breach, she replied, "I done deliver all the babies on the Caye. I never lost a mother or a child. If we had a breach baby, we found two strong men.

They picked the mother up by the ankles and gently shook her until the baby turned around." I later heard the same story from other Caribbean women.

I became absorbed in writing, but something in the back of my mind was still telling me to think about finding my own place to live. I liked Dallas, but I did not want to settle there. I always considered New Jersey my true home and was leaning towards moving back there.

It had been too long since I had seen my parents and my two sisters. When I was seven years old, my mother and father divorced, which was unusual in the 1950's. Up until then, I had never heard of divorce. My mother explained to me one night, before I went to sleep, that she and Daddy did not love one another anymore, but they both still loved us. It was a pivotal moment for me and I remember it clearly.

My mother was a teacher, first in Special Education, then she taught first grade for many years. When she passed, some of her first-grade students sent messages about how she had changed their lives. In fact, at her memorial service, there were many people that I did not know. Several people who attended told me that if it was not for her, they would not still be here. She was very outspoken, as I well know, and never hesitated to tell someone when he or she was out of line.

A few years before my mother died, we were having lunch and she told me that she always believed in me. I realized then, that she had been my saving grace. She believed in me when I did not always believe in myself. It was a blessing.

My father dropped out of high school to join the Army in World War II. After the divorce, he went on to get a master's degree in Psychology and worked as a high school guidance counselor, until he was 73 years old. As I pursued a more focused spiritual path, so did he. Well into his 80's, he devoured all the New Age books I could find for him. He told me many times that I had changed his life.

My father was truly the wisest person I have known. One day, as we sat in the sun on a park bench, he told me that moderation is the highest human state. It took me a while to realize how profound that statement was, and it inspired me to write a forthcoming book entitled Balance and Moderation. He was always wondering about things. So many times, I heard him say, *I wonder how they do that,* or *I wonder why they do it this way.*

I have had many teachers and guides that have escorted me through the phases of my life, parents, friends, lovers, and even strangers. I am grateful to all of them. At times, it was painful, but that is what it took. My wish is that I can do the same for someone else.

In September, I decided to take a trip to New Jersey. I wanted to be there during autumn, my favorite season. I also intended to look for a place to live. About a week before I was to fly, the phone rang.

"Hi Wendy, it's Rose, gal. Da wadda gowan?" she asked in Creole.

"Rose, how are you? How are the kids?"

"We are all well. I wanted to tell you that Samosa and Lisa have moved to Switzerland for good. She decided to take him there to rehab both of them. They have been gone for a month. I know you want to come back to the island and we all miss you."

"Rose that is good news, for Sam and for me. Maybe I will come back. Thanks for letting me know."

I had not learned about dowsing yet; so, there was only one thing to do, flip a coin to see whether to go to New Jersey to live, or back to Caye Caulker. Heads New Jersey, tails Belize. Tails it was. I first flew to New Jersey to see my family for a few weeks and then flew back to the island. Another turn up the spiral...

Back in Paradise

"I'm sorry, Wendy," said Rico, "I have rented the house on a permanent basis."

"Don't worry, Rico, it is probably better that I start fresh in a new house."

"You left at the right time. Samosa was a real mess. He is only lucky that girl took him away. Why don't you check with Miss Ilna, across the street? I believe she has an apartment for rent in that cement house she built."

"Thanks, Rico, I'll do that."

The apartment, right on the beach, was available and I rented it. It was the perfect place for me. It even had a refrigerator. The kitchen window, which faced the street, had red hibiscus blossoms growing right outside, which hummingbirds frequented in the morning. Palm trees shaded the front of the house, which was about twenty yards from the sea, and the heavenly, cool breeze blew most of the time.

I became friendly with a man from England that was staying in one of the small cabana rentals next door. John Byrne was his name. We had some interesting talks about Crop Circles in the United Kingdom. He taught me how to make silk screens for creating designs on t-shirts. There was no one selling hand painted t-shirts at the time, so I thought it would be a diversion, and a way to make a little money as well.

I have never been much of an artist, but I do have an eye for beauty. The solution came to me on a shopping trip to Belize City. I bought a few coloring books to get the designs I wanted, including a mermaid, several fish, and a few tropical landscapes. I found all the basic supplies I needed in Belize City and ordered more t-shirt paint and silkscreen fabric from the States. Luckily, t-shirts were one thing manufactured in Belize, a country that imports almost everything. The Belizean t-shirts were good quality cotton and the company delivered them to the island via the tourist boat. The house where I was living had a fence on the street side. Each day I would hang a few shirts there to advertise. I was enjoying the diversion of creating t-shirt art and painting the colorful designs, but I had no idea how popular they would be. Soon I could not make enough. My little life there was quite perfect.

A New Friend

One particularly fine morning, as I was walking home from the market, I met Rose.

"Wendy, do you remember the woman from Canada, named Bev, the one that Samosa was seeing behind your back?" she asked.

"Yes Rose, thanks for reminding me," I replied.

"She is back on the island. Look, there she is right now," she continued, oblivious to my subtly sarcastic reply, "see her down at the end of the street with the white shirt and blonde hair?"

"Yes, I see her," I said.

I did not recognize the woman, but I never had a good look at her when the affair was happening.

A few days later, I woke up before the sun had risen. I pulled on some clothes and stepped out on to the beach, in front of my apartment. As I stood there, I had one of the most profound moments of my adult life, one that clearly remains in my conscious awareness. As I felt the cool sand under my bare feet, I began to meld into the Earth, becoming one with it, and part of it. The Goddess Energy of Gaia flowed up through the bottoms of my feet, into my whole body, and out the top of my head. It then surrounded and enveloped me. I was having the experience of being an authentic, natural, female human being, alive on the planet, nothing more. If only for a few moments I was completely free of all thoughts and cares. It was a true starting point, with a clear energetic slate.

As I returned to the world around me, I knew that I had created the freedom that I had just experienced. I was proud of myself for doing so. It was empowering. Even to this day, I can experience the connection I had with Gaia on that beautiful morning.

After an inspirational start to my day, it was time to get to work. I was hanging my t-shirts on the fence, when I saw Bev approaching. I still did not remember ever seeing her, but I thought I would clear the air, since the island was so small and everyone knew everyone else, and all that went on.

"Good morning," she said, as she passed.

"Hello, are you Bev? You're from Canada, right?" I asked.

"Yes, I am, and you are?" she replied.

In my life, I have stuck my foot in my mouth many times, but this time it actually paid off. "My name is Wendy, listen, no hard feelings."

"No hard feelings for what?" she asked, looking honestly confused.

"Didn't you have an affair with Samosa, the last time you were here? Listen, he and I broke up, so no hard feelings."

She looked at me and started laughing. "Samosa? Actually, he would probably be the last man on Earth with whom I would have taken up. When I met him, he was drunk all the time and with some awful Swiss girl, with blonde dreadlocks."

"Ooops," I said, "I guess there is more than one Bev from Canada." We both laughed and have been best friends ever since.

Bev lived in Toronto and worked as a Production Coordinator in the film industry. She was blonde and beautiful, both in body and spirit. She reminded me of a combination of Marilyn Monroe and Mae West. When she was between projects, she liked to vacation on the Caye.

She began to stop by my house each day, while I painted t-shirts, to say hello and chat. We discovered that we both had the same irreverent sense of humor. We talked and laughed until our bellies hurt. After a couple of weeks, she offered to help me paint, just for something to do. As we worked, she told me about her life, which had been fascinating, but I will not tell her story here. That is her job, and I hope she tells it someday.

As I got to know Bev more, I felt safe in her company, safe enough to speak of things I had been holding inside for too long. One afternoon, she asked me about my life and what brought me to Caye Caulker. I talked a bit about my childhood and how I ended up at the University of Oklahoma. Then I began to tell her about the affair that changed my life.

"The first time I saw Jim was in March of 1971, in Norman, Oklahoma. He was sitting on the sidewalk, leaning up against the wall of Ernie's Town Tavern, a local restaurant on Campus Corner, the small area of restaurants and shops in the two-block square business district that catered to the needs of the university community. Jim was shirtless, wearing a pair of cutoff jeans, and holding a transistor radio with a wire hanger antenna, up to his ear. He was handsome and tan, with brown, sun-bleached hair.

As I walked by, he said hello. I smiled and kept walking. That was the first time I saw him. After that, when I went to Campus Corner, I often saw Jim sitting in the same spot. I thought him a bit wild, so I ignored him, unless I thought he wasn't looking."

"Yes," said Bev, "back in college, all it took was a cute smile for a guy to be a good choice. We lived in the moment and let passion rule. So, what happened to change your mind? I assume you did change your mind."

"You assume correctly, but it is all about timing. Back then I was a very cute twenty-three-year-old graduate student. Two months prior, I had broken up with my boyfriend of four years, and was living in adult student housing for the rest of the semester.

Sunday, April 4, 1971 was a drizzly, dreary day in Norman. I woke up early and went to Campus Corner in search of breakfast. The only place open was Liberty Drug, a soda fountain that had not changed a bit since the 1950's. It could have been the set for Happy Days, with its counter and round stools, covered in red leather, and booths in the back. Originally, it was a drug store and then a soda fountain.

The elderly owner and pharmacist was the only one there when I walked in. I ordered tea and toast and sat in one of the booths, in luxurious silence. I was still shocked by the death of one of the students that had jumped out of the window of a high-rise dorm a few days earlier. Oddly enough, the same week as the incident, I had made an assignment for my students, in the

English composition class that I was teaching, to write an essay on the Simon and Garfunkel song, Save the Life of My Child. The song told of a mother watching her son on a ledge, contemplating jumping to his death. One of my students had not written a good assignment all semester. After seeing the boy as he jumped, he wrote a stellar essay, and as a result, found his confidence as a writer.

As I sipped my tea, I wondered why the boy did it. Had he found the courage to jump, or lost the courage to live. I later learned that his girlfriend had recently broken up with him, which was a clue. Before I could think about it anymore, the door opened and Jim walked in. He bought the Sunday paper, looked back and saw me sitting in the booth, and left. About five minutes went by, the door opened again, and he was back, walking to where I sat.

He asked if he could join me and I said okay. He seemed a bit less eccentric, with a shirt on. He introduced himself and asked what I was doing there so early in the morning. I explained that it was almost ten o'clock, which was not very early, unless one had been out partying the night before, which I had not. We talked for a couple of hours and I told him a little about my life. He said that he had been a high school math teacher, but dropped out.

In 1971, a segment of the university-focused population lived in a liberal oasis, surrounded by Oklahoma conservatism. The neighborhood attracted many local hippies. They lived relatively unhindered and protected by the campus and surrounding area, where very few native Norman residents ventured. It was the psychedelic era. Marijuana, LSD, magic mushrooms, and peyote were available, and minds were opening. Of course, the main danger was getting caught smoking marijuana. Back then, many a young man was sentenced to up to seven years in prison for one joint.

The rain stopped and Jim asked me if I wanted to go for a walk. We spent the day strolling around the campus and talking. He told me I was beautiful. No man had ever said that to me. In fact, even though my parents had told me many times, I did not have that image of myself. Today I see many beautiful women and I often wonder if they believe that they are. At the end of the day, Jim gave me his address and we went our separate ways.

I did not know many people at the University. My ex-boyfriend and I had mostly kept to ourselves, and when we separated, I was on my own. Scott had drastically changed during the course of our relationship. We first met when I was in my second year at Monmouth College, in West Long Branch, New Jersey. I was sharing an apartment with three other girls and he came over with a friend. It was love at first sight, or at least something at first sight. Everything was happy for a couple of years, but over time, he changed. He became set in his ways and expected me to adhere to his changes. We grew apart and we separated, but he thought, as many do, that he could win me back.

One afternoon, he met me after my classes and asked if I wanted to have dinner. I guess I felt sorry for him, or thought we could just be friends, so I said ok. He came to pick me up at my dorm at six o'clock and we rode off on our bicycles toward the restaurant. When we got to the traffic light at Campus Corner, it changed to orange and he sped through. I stopped as the light turned red and looked across at his smirking face, happy with himself that he had won some sort of victory. I realized at that moment he would never understand that it was not a competition between us."

"So, then what happened?" Bev asked. "Did you wait for the light to change back to green?"

"No, I still had the card Jim had given me with his address. I quickly turned left and did not look back. Jim's apartment was upstairs in a wooden house in the part of town where Okies lived. It was a lovely, quiet neighborhood, with lots of trees. I rang the bell and he came down the stairs to open the door.

"Well, well, well," he said, when he saw me. I went upstairs to his apartment. That weekend was the beginning of our affair. Our relationship was a meeting of the minds. Jim was smart and so am I. He was a charmer and I had never been charmed.

At first, we continued as we were, I was still living at the dorm and teaching at the University, and he sat on Campus Corner with his radio. At that time, I was not certain for what purpose he sat there every day, but when one is young, and believes they are in love, everything seems to make sense. Jim, like many young people of that era, wanted to change the world. Moreover, he believed he could. Now that I think back, having me in his life, allowed him to believe that he could accomplish great things. It was years later before I realized my own strength and power, and how easily I could give it away.

By the end of the school term, we were living together. He wrote original songs, played the guitar, and I sang. I discovered that I had an excellent singing voice, with quite a range. We became a musical duo, playing our songs on Campus Corner.

I did not have grand dreams back then, receiving a master's degree was about as far as mine went. Jim, on the other hand, had an image of himself, as a sort of Avatar, which to him meant the world owed him riches and fame. The attraction for me was being with someone who was a free thinker.

We both decided to leave Oklahoma to pursue his dream of becoming rock stars, which had also become my dream. It seemed that the logical place to do that was California, so off we went to San Francisco to become street musicians. We played every day at Powell and Market Streets, where the cable car turns around. Jim believed that someone passing by, would discover us, but that did not happen.

After a couple of years, I began to see him getting frustrated, not knowing how to proceed towards his goal of becoming successful. There was no going back to the straight life, after all, it was the Hippie Generation, and we were living in it. Jim's determination to become famous, had replaced our love affair. Finally, it became clear that something must be done. He proposed that we separate for a while, so we could find ourselves. Apparently, he felt lost. I did not, but I agreed."

* * *

"Where did you go, and what did you do?" Bev asked.

"During the twenty-one months that we were separated, I travelled a bit. I spend a year in Livingston, Montana, working as a substitute high school teacher. The beauty of the mountains lured me into staying there; however, the winter was a deal breaker. The wind whipped through the valley most of the time, making the cold even more unbearable. It was a common expression in Livingston, if the wind ever stopped blowing, that people would fall flat on their face. One February morning I turned on the weather report, only to learn that the wind chill factor was minus sixty degrees. It was time to leave.

I decided to take a trip back to Norman, where it was warmer. A few days after I arrived, an old friend informed me that Jim was living in San Francisco. He was still a street musician and was eager to see me. I was not sure if I wanted to see him after all that time. In essentials, I had not changed. I was the same as I had always been.

I presume that I was meant to learn some more lessons, because I decided to go to San Francisco and see him. I considered that choice as the road to non-conformity. The collective consciousness was not for me. Even though that path took me on a rocky road for quite some time, in the end it paid off. It led me to a better life than I could have imagined.

After only a few days in San Francisco, I saw that Jim had changed, there was no doubt about it. He was even more unhappy than he was before. He could not believe that I had stayed away so long. I reminded him that it was his idea to separate. I am not sure if I felt sorry for him, was still in love with him, or believed I was meant to follow through on this path. Whatever I was thinking at the time, or perhaps not thinking, I stayed. I enjoyed making music and I embraced the freedom of the life we were living. In addition to original music, we played songs from the 50's and 60's. In the process of buying old 45 rpm records to get lyrics for songs to arrange and perform, we became aware that some records were collectible and more valuable than others.

A month after I arrived in California, I discovered I was pregnant by a young man I had been seeing in Montana. We had separated under very unpleasant circumstances. His friends convinced him that I was not suitable for him and he bent under the pressure. When I discovered I was carrying his baby, I had no desire to tell him. Of course, Jim knew the baby was not his, but was willing to raise the child as his own.

In my third month, we took a trip in his van to start searching for collectable records in thrift stores and flea markets. We were camping one night in the beautiful mountains near Lake Tahoe, when I awoke in the middle of the night in a lot of pain. I was losing the baby. He took me to the hospital, where I stayed for a couple of days.

During the time I was recovering, I decided that I did not want to be a street musician anymore. I was satisfied to play music for my own enjoyment. I made it clear to Jim that I was resigning from the band. He accepted my decision and suggested we start a business buying and selling rare phonograph records. I thought it sounded like a good plan.

We bought a few collectible record price guidebooks and began to travel around, in search of used records. The western United States had not been explored by record dealers, as had other parts of the country, so we amassed a large inventory in just a few months. We started going to record conventions to wheel and deal. In a few years, we became well-known collectors and dealers.

Bev, I must be boring you, talking about myself."

"No, please continue, I want to hear the rest of the story and how you ended up here. Let me go buy some stout and then we can resume."

Major Life Events

A few minutes later, Bev returned with four bottles of the dark brew. I was glad, because I knew I would need a drink to continue the story. The difficult part was coming up.

"In 1978, I became pregnant again," I said, as I continued my story. "The prospect of a baby made us both happy. I was thrilled at the thought of being a mother. However, there was a complication, the baby was breech. The doctor informed me that if the baby did not turn on its own as the due date got closer, they would perform a cesarean. We were in Oklahoma, when I went into labor early, during an ice storm. There was black ice everywhere, making it impossible to drive or even for an ambulance to get to me. By the time I reached the hospital, it was too late to perform the operation; the baby was already being born. My bones were too small for the baby's head, and he suffocated.

I remember waking from the anesthesia and asking the nurse, "where's my baby?"

"He died," she replied.

I sunk back into the painless, drugged sleep. When I finally woke up again, they brought him in for me to see. He was a beautiful baby boy, with black hair and a face like mine. His name was Jamie."

"Oh Wendy, I am so sorry," said Bev.

"Thanks," I replied, tears welling up in my eyes. I stopped talking for a few minutes, until I composed myself. Then I continued.

"By 1984, it was getting difficult to find records. We no longer had a profitable business. Jim was even more depressed than ever and taking it out on me. In July of that year, he decided that he wanted to go to Palenque, Mexico. He believed that taking magic mushrooms would help to overcome his deep seeded unhappiness. Since the world was not giving him the abundance and success he wanted, he was beginning to realize that perhaps he had been mistaken to have expected it.

To be honest, Bev, I was sorry he could not be happy, but I knew there was no longer anything I could do to help him, he had to help himself. I agreed to go with him to Mexico, but I had made up my mind that after we returned, I was going to leave him for good.

The next part is one I have not spoken of, to anyone, but I believe it is time. We drove through Mexico, on the way to Palenque, and camped in the van at night. I had not realized how truly unhappy Jim was, until the first night of the trip, when he told me that he did not want to live anymore. That was the be careful what you wish for moment in his life.

Three days into the journey, we were driving through Oaxaca. We miscalculated how long it would take to reach our destination and it was late by the time we reached the town. We couldn't find a campground, so we stopped at a rest area on the side of the road.

In the middle of the night, we were awakened by a knock on the window. Jim got out and began talking to some men. Then he got back in the vehicle and told me that they wanted to see our IDs. The next thing I knew, he started the van. As he reached for the gearshift lever, to put it in reverse, four shots were fired at point-blank range, killing him instantly.

I began to cry out for help, but no one was there, except the men surrounding the van. I moved up into the passenger seat, from the back of the van where we had been sleeping. I was screaming hysterically. I saw that there were about eight men outside the vehicle. One man pulled me out and hit me in the back of my head, with the butt of his gun, to shut me up. It was at that moment that I audibly heard a voice from someone that was not physically there. The voice said, very clearly, if you panic, you will surely die. I became calm.

Looking back, I know I was in an altered state. Higher Beings were protecting me and even though I was in life-threatening danger, I felt that I would be all right. Two of the men took me into one of the cars, and the rest of the men followed in other vehicles. The same voice then said, no matter what happens, do not let them see your fear. Then it said, get rid of the others.

In Spanish, I suggested to the driver, a man with a pockmarked face, that he get rid of his friends, so he and I could go have a drink somewhere. I was trying to act as casual as possible. It worked, he told the others something I could not hear, leaving only two of them and me. I asked them who they were and what they wanted. They said they were police from up North. What they wanted was *sexo con una gringa*. I realized I was the gringa. They drove down a dirt road and both had their way with me at gunpoint. Then they took me back to the main road and told me to get out.

As they pulled off, the passenger pointed his pistol out the window towards me, and I quickly got behind the car, so he couldn't shoot me. They sped off and left me there. I was barefoot, but I ran out about a hundred yards into the field, in case they came back. I sat down on the ground, still in a state of shock, unable to even think about all that had just happened.

It was at that moment, when I should have been wildly hysterical, that I looked up at the sky, and had one of the most profound moments of my life. It was very dark. There was no Moon. The sky was filled with more stars than I ever thought was possible. I had never seen such a site and I was in awe. I stayed transfixed on the night sky, the same one that people have watched since the dawn of humanity. Somehow, it was drawing the pain and terror, of what I had just experienced, out of me. I became one with the beauty and majesty of creation. I merged with the stars, I felt the presence of those that were watching over me, and I once again became aware of my connection with the Star Beings.

After about an hour, I felt composed enough to stand back up and walk. I had to try and get back to the vehicle. I knew I was on the same road where we had parked the van, but I was also aware that it was at least fifteen miles away. I would have to hitch a ride. I could see a house with a light, about a quarter of a mile in the distance. The van was in the other direction, but I thought I might get some help there. I walked back to the road, but suddenly it occurred to me that the men had taken off towards that house, and there was a chance they might be there. I turned around and walked the other way, towards the van.

My feet were beginning to hurt, but I continued to walk on the road, hoping a bus or truck would come along. Each time I saw a car, I hid, in case the men returned. Finally, a bus approached and I stepped into the road to flag it down, but it kept going. About forty-five minutes later, another bus came. It was beginning to get light by then. This time they stopped and I got in. I explained to the driver what had happened and he did not ask me for money."

"Good Lord, Wendy, how horrible," said Bev, "you poor thing."

"Yes, it was rather awful. At least I speak Spanish, or it could have been worse. In fact, the whole thing could have been a lot worse."

"It most certainly could have," Bev replied. "So, then what happened?"

"The bus arrived at the spot where the van was parked. There were about a dozen local residents looking at Jim's body inside the vehicle. The driver stopped and a few of the men walked over to the van. None of them would help me move the body out of the driver's seat. The bus driver explained that I had better first go to the police station. I grabbed my shoes, backpack, and got all the money and travel documents out of Jim's bag, then I continued, with the bus, into town, where I went to the police station.

The police officer drove me back to the scene and moved the body into the passenger seat, so I could drive the van back to the station. When I got there, a Mexican woman kindly invited me to stay at her house. She and her daughters cleaned out the van. There was blood everywhere. They were very gracious and washed all my clothes as well.

Then they helped me bury Jim's body in the local cemetery. After the funeral, they left me alone at the gravesite to say goodbye. I thought about the thirteen years that Jim had been in my life. As I stood on the hill surrounded by trees and flowers, I felt his presence there with me. He was finally happy and I felt the love that he had for me, the love he was unable to show while he was alive. It was closure, and it was good.

I could not legally sell the van in Mexico, or I would have done so and flown back. The next morning, I began the long drive back to the United States. The police had called the American Embassy in Mexico City. They asked that I stop there on the way back. Finding the Embassy was difficult. At one point, I made a U-turn and was pulled over by the Mexico City police. I explained I was going to the Embassy and the police officer said he would ride with me to show me the way. His partner would follow in the patrol car.

As he went back to inform the other officer, I instinctively and quickly took out $40 and put it in my pocket. Then I shoved my wallet, with more than $1000 in cash, into the crack in the seat. The officer came back and began to direct me. After about ten minutes, it became clear that we were not going to the Embassy. I had studied the map beforehand and I knew I had been very close. I pulled the money out of my pocket, handed it to him, and said, *"embajada, por favor"*.

We arrived at the Embassy shortly after that. The American Embassy worker was not very sympathetic. In fact, in the middle of my story, he answered the phone, and while I sat there and waited, he chatted with someone about lunch. They gave me some papers and I was again on my way.

When I reached the border in Laredo, the immigration officer asked me, how long I had been in Mexico, and what I was bringing back. I explained that I had been there for two weeks and had brought back nothing. Then he asked me to get out of the vehicle. I handed him the papers from the Mexican police and the Embassy and said, 'My boyfriend was shot to death, and I was raped at gunpoint'."

"Go on through," he replied, handing me back my papers.

"Jeez, you must have been glad to get back to the US," said Bev.

"You know it. I drove into Laredo and stayed at a nice hotel. I was exhausted. The van never started again. It seems the engine was shot, no pun intended," I said, trying to inject a little humor into the tragic mood I had created with my story. "I took a taxi to the airport and flew to New Jersey to stay with my family for a while. Of course, they were shocked and sorry about it all, but glad Jim was out of my life.

He was one of my important life teachers, but I am sorry to say that I felt relieved more than sad. I had learned how easy it is to lose one's self in a relationship. When that happens, the love affair is doomed."

That was enough storytelling for one day. We opened the second bottle of stout and toasted to the future.

* * *

"So, what did you do in New Jersey?" Bev asked, the following day.

"I stayed there for a few months. I liquidated some investments that I inherited from my grandparents, spent time recovering from my ordeal, and enjoyed time with my family. I was rather jumpy though. I could not watch anything violent on TV or in a movie, especially if there were guns. By November, I decided that the only way to overcome the fear I was experiencing, was to face it. I decided to go back to Mexico. After all, I surmised, thousands of people travel there every year and return unharmed. In December, I flew to Mexico City and then took the bus to San Cristóbal de las Casas."

I continued to relay the story of how I traveled to the Caye and met Samosa. "I thought I had learned my lesson about men, but it seems I had a bit more to learn. Sam was my next teacher. He had so many good traits. I overlooked the bad ones as long as I could. In retrospect, I realize that each of us does the best we can, with what we have, to work with at the time.

"When did you discover he was cheating?" Bev asked.

"One day Sam went on a sailing trip with about twelve tourists. By the time they came back, the weather had turned very stormy. One thing I can say about him, he was an amazing captain. During the storm, he had the sense to sail the boat into a shallow place near the end of the island. If he had tried to dock the boat, it might have crashed into the pier. The passengers were able to get off the sailboat and wade to the shore. I have given him credit for his actions, but one of the passengers informed me that he had been drinking quite a bit.

That night he stayed with the sailboat. The next morning, I rode my bike down the beach until I could see the boat, which was still in the shoal. I asked a fisherman to take me out there in his dory. When I boarded the boat, there was Samosa, still asleep, with a young blonde tourist by his side. I uttered an array of expletives, which of course woke them both. I left in the dory, which was still waiting, and went home to pack his things.

When Sam returned later I told him to get out, although I did not say it quite so nicely. You know what, Bev, he managed to talk me out of it, convincing me that he still loved me and that it would never happen again. It was at that moment, when I agreed he could stay, that I reached a low point in my emotional life. I felt like a puddle. The good news is, from there, I could only go up.

Yes, I stayed a little while longer, but it was never the same, not only because I caught him cheating, which would have been enough to spoil any relationship, but because the trust was gone. Once that happens, it is truly the end. The departure date may be delayed, but the entity, which is the relationship, has dissolved into thin air. In any event, that was only the beginning of a string of his bad behavior, which only made me realize that I never really knew him at all. I only knew the man I wanted him to be, and the man he chose to reveal.

So here I am, happy and single. This is the time of my life when I am getting to know myself, although I don't know how much longer I am going to stay on the island. I am getting bored painting t-shirts. It feels less artistic and more like factory work each passing day."

I have an idea, Wendy. Would you like to come and work with me on a film? You would have to come to Toronto."

"Certainly, I would! That would be great. Part of the reason I am still here is because I have not quite decided where to go or what to do when I get there."

"How are your computer skills?" she asked.

"They are rather non-existent, but I have wanted to learn how to use a computer, ever since I saw the woman in the travel agency here, using her computer as if it were second nature to her."

"Ok, listen," said Bev, "I am going to leave you the laptop I brought with me, so you can become familiar with using it. I have another one at home. I just bought this refurbished one to bring with me to Belize. You can type some of the things you have written into the computer and save them there. Then I will send you a book that will help you learn a program that you will need to know for the job. The program is already installed on the laptop."

"Thank you, Bev, you are so kind."

"You are most welcome, but there is some selfish motivation going on here. You are smart, I see how you work, and I would like to have someone like you to work along with me. You speak your true feelings, no drama. That is not easy to find in a person these days."

"Well, I'm from New Jersey, we get right down to it." We both laughed.

"Once you have become more computer savvy, I will apply for a work permit for you to come as my assistant. It might take a few months, but I think I can arrange it."

I felt as though I was going up the spiral again

Canada, Aye

Bev finished another project in nine months and then came back to the Caye for a break. By then, I had gone through the book she had sent me and was quite proficient on the computer. It seemed to come naturally to me.

"I am hoping for another job to start in about two months," Bev said, "it's a children's TV show. If you would like to work on it, you would be the Assistant Production Coordinator."

"Great, I accept your offer," I replied.

Two and a half months later, I was living in a studio apartment in the lovely Portuguese neighborhood, west of downtown Toronto.

The children's TV show had actors, puppets, and animation. The set was full of antique toys, belonging to the producer. The puppeteers had to work in extremely cramped conditions under a counter, where the puppets sat in the toy store set. During the breaks, they would make us laugh, using the puppets to make rude jokes.

I worked on a few more shows, including Finding Forrester, with Sean Connery. By then, Bev was married and had two children, my godchildren. The next film was to be shot in France. When we arrived in Nice, we discovered that the production company was not going to pay for her to have an assistant, so I agreed to stay as nanny for the children. Three months, living in a villa on the French Riviera, and spending time with my lovely godchildren, was not a bad job at all.

Full Circle

Upon our return to Toronto, we started a project that ended up folding before shooting even started. Then Bev discovered that it was going to be almost impossible for me to have another work permit. I decided it was time to go back to New Jersey. I signed up for some advanced database classes, in hopes of getting a job in Information Technology. In the meantime, I accepted a job as a Software Support Specialist in a company in Parsippany, New Jersey.

I met Harry at a company sponsored computer class. We ate lunch together during the break and he asked for my e-mail address. A year later, we were married. I will not go into the details of the relationship, except that after two years, it ended in divorce.

Harry's home computer was networked to mine. One day, while searching for a file on my computer, I navigated to a shared folder and found another folder he had saved there. The folder contained e-mails and messages from women he had been seeing, while he was supposed to be working late. When I married him, I explained that if he did anything untoward, it would only be once; there would be no second chances. Apparently, he didn't think I meant it. When I discovered what he was up to, I filed for divorce. There is nothing special about that story, but what happened afterwards, changed the direction of my life.

I was devastated about the breakup. I thought we had been so much in love, silly me. I came home from work on Valentine's Day and he was gone, moved out, and the key was on my desk. I was relieved, heartbroken, and in physical pain, so much that it was difficult for me to walk. My father told me the pain was all due to Harry. I knew he was right.

A couple of months later, I was at work, when a friend asked me why I was limping. I explained that, for some reason, my legs were very painful.

"Why don't you get some Reiki?" she replied. "My sister is a Reiki practitioner in India. According to her, it really helps."

"What's Reiki?" I asked.

She explained that it was an energy healing technique. I was immediately drawn to finding out more. The next weekend I booked a Reiki session for myself at the Omega Institute for Holistic Studies in Rhinebeck, New York. My father had always been intrigued by Reflexology, so I also booked a Reflexology session for him.

The Reiki session was relaxing, and afterwards I felt less pain. In addition, during the session, I became consciously aware of my Energy Body. I liked the feeling, for it was new and clear. I was opening to a new awareness and it was exciting.

I knew it would take more than one session, to heal the pain I was experiencing. Shortly afterwards, I learned that if I had a Reiki attunement, I could give Reiki to myself. I calculated the price of one Reiki session and the price of a class. It was a simple choice; I would learn Reiki and heal myself.

On a weekend in New York City, I took the Reiki I and II classes. My excellent teacher, Kathie Lipinski is a very spiritual, grounded, and enlightened person. During a meditation, I met some of the Spirit Guides, Ascended Masters, and Archangels that I would be working with for the rest of my life. My mind had been opened to multidimensionality and I would never be the same again.

I gave myself a Reiki session every night. After a few months, I was nearly recovered. As the pain subsided, I was also able to begin a Yoga practice. By the time I took the Reiki Master class, a year later, I was physically healed, had lost twenty pounds, and was discovering my intuitive connection to the universe. It was the start of my formal spiritual journey. I say formal, because I was always on a spiritual path, as is everyone, but now I was consciously embracing my journey on the infinite spiral of life.

As a child, I often wondered if I was awake or dreaming. I believed that when I went to sleep, I would truly wake up and find myself somewhere else. I was beginning to believe that I had finally woken up, and had found that somewhere else. I had taken a quantum leap up the spiral.

The new frontier is the unexplored realm of expanding consciousness. I knew that other people took for granted what I was just discovering, but I am also aware that I have a curious and innovative spirit, which instinctively reaches out to the unknown.

A year after I took Reiki Master training, I went on to take Karuna Reiki. Since then, I have developed my own system of Reiki, called Merkeba Reiki. It uses Metatron's Cube, embellished with Sacred Geometric shapes, along with other Reiki symbols. The geometric aspect acts as an energetic regulator for the Reiki energy coming through.

I began to study many different esoteric modalities, including working with crystals and Archangels, but what resonated the most with me was Sacred Geometry, as the bridge between science, mathematics, and spirituality. Geometry has been a major focus of my spiritual journey. It encompasses a degree of perfection, to excuse the oxymoron. Sacred Geometry creates an energy that has resonance with source, and in the Third Dimension, it expresses the creative nature of energy as number and shape.

I read as many spiritual books as I could, and took from them what resonated with me. I shared many of the books with my father, who even well into his 80's also enjoyed them. After reading the Four Agreements, he told me that Don Miguel Ruiz was his guru.

On the morning of July 12, 2008, I drove to his home to pick him up and take him out for breakfast. I was looking forward to another one of our stimulating, philosophical discussions. When I arrived, I found that he had died that morning, while washing the dishes. The water was still running. It was a sad loss.

My father was never ill. He had a cabinet full of supplements in the kitchen and relied on natural methods to keep him healthy. He introduced me to the benefits of Apple Cider Vinegar, Oil of Oregano, and other such natural cures. He did not like going to the doctor. "Once they get you in their clutches...," he would say. I find I have a similar belief, to the chagrin of some that know me. I find it incomprehensible that so many people, in what is supposed to be the most advanced country in the world, are unwell. That does not seem very advanced to me. There, I have said it!

My father was a Walking Master, the legacy he passed on to me. Now he is an Ascended Master.

My parents had been divorced for more than fifty years, but when my mother heard of my father's death, I saw a part of her go as well. Six months later, she also passed away. She was not as open to alternative healing methods as my father was, but one day I went to visit her and found that, from coughing, she had pulled a muscle on her side.

"Mom," I said, "why don't you let me give you some Reiki. I do not even have to touch you. It can't hurt."

She agreed, and I gave her Reiki for about a half hour, which seemed to alleviate her pain. After that breakthrough, when I went to her house, I always asked if she wanted a bit of Reiki. She was beginning to like it and welcomed my offers. She stayed in her recliner for each session and when I finished, she would say, "that was delicious".

I am so grateful that I had the opportunity to share my gifts with my parents. I know that they both left this lifetime with a higher vibration. To me, that is the best accomplishment anyone can achieve.

As a child, when I was unwell, my mother would tell me, "I wish I could be sick for you." Throughout her life, she had many different illnesses. To some extent, she recovered from all of them.

My mother lived in the energy of Mary Magdalene. She was a Bodhisattva who took on the suffering that her children might have otherwise endured.

About three weeks after her passing, I attended an Astrology class. When the instructor looked at my chart, she asked me if a major event had occurred in my life recently. I explained that my mother had passed that month. She studied the chart a bit more and informed me that it was a very auspicious time for her to go.

My father once told me, "a man always loves his first wife." I began to realize that when we are connected to someone on one level, even if we do not spend our entire life with them, the connection always remains. Amongst my father's possessions was a small glass bird. Amongst my mother's possessions was also a small glass bird. Both birds now sit on a table in front of my balcony window, looking out over the horizon. Whenever I am out and about, and see two birds together, I know that my mother and father are watching over me.

Spirituality

I continued to learn different healing techniques, and attended lectures and events related to spiritual growth. I noticed that some classes were fascinating when I took them, but over time I moved on to something else. Looking back, I see how one pursuit led to another and began to steer me on an accelerated path of enlightenment and ascension.

In October of 2010, I met two women that were going to the Earth-Keeper 10-10-10 event, in Arkansas. Unfortunately, the event was already sold out when I tried to buy a ticket, so I signed up for the live stream, which would broadcast two days of speakers.

At one point, the entire group did a meditation, outside of the mountain lodge where the event was held. I was lying on the sofa in my living room, with my eyes closed, when I became aware that I was etherically floating above the circle of people in Arkansas. I stayed there until the meditation was over, then gently floated back to my body.

I was so inspired by the speakers at the event, particularly James *Tyberonn*, the founder of Earth-Keeper, who channels Archangel Metatron, that I signed up for his online class called, The Metatronic Keys. It was a life changer. I began to feel the energy of Archangel Metatron becoming a more prevalent influence in my life.

I was beginning to tune into the presence of Angels and Ascended Masters. My energy is of the Violet Ray, so it was natural that I began working with Saint Germain. The first time I met him was when I was ill with pneumonia. He came etherically in a vision, which might have been a dream. He had long brown hair, with wooden ornaments woven into it, reaching past his waist. He sat cross-legged on the floor and said that he would always be watching over me.

My connection with Quan Yin began when I took Karuna Reiki. Archangel Michael has been protecting me all along. When I communicate with them, I can hear their answers clearly in my mind.

These types of experiences are common among spiritual seekers, but when one first becomes aware of the possibilities that exist, it is more than marvelous. However, care must be taken, not to become a spiritual snob. Occurrences, such as meeting one's guides, normally happen in the early stages of a conscious spiritual path. As one proceeds towards a more esoteric level of spirituality, the elementary experiences should not be minimized. They are an important piece of one's spiritual foundation.

Rational, logical, deductive thinking has been a sort of prison for modern humanity. Before it became almost absolute reality, there existed a connection with what lies beyond. Indigenous people have not forgotten this, and those discovering spirituality are once again remembering.

Channeling is the process of receiving information from outside the realm of linear thinking. The information may be from higher beings, the Higher Self, or the energy of the Universe. Most people channel without even realizing it, they get a feeling or hunch about something. Perhaps they get an idea, which will solve a problem, not knowing the source of their inspiration.

I began receiving esoteric information, which I wrote down as it came through. All knowledge already exists, it must only be discovered or recalled. Therefore, when one invents something, such as the telephone, the concept of it has always existed, but it can only be discovered when the time is right.

The same goes for spiritual knowledge, it makes its appearance at the appropriate time. This explains why many channels and spiritual authors often bring through similar messages at the same time. The particular theme comes through each of them but is presented to the world in various ways.

In 2008, I published my first book, Do You Want to Be Happy NOW? By 2010, I published a second book, Life is Good, All is Well - Everything is Vibration.

In 2011, I went on the Sacred Britain Pilgrimage, with the Earth-Keeper group. I had no idea how strong my Celtic roots were until I landed in England.

I am a Jane Austen fan, so I decided to arrive a few days early, and go on a Jane Austen tour before the Earth-Keeper trip began. I chose Hidden Britain Tours, and had a personal guide who took me to places that inspired Jane Austen's works. I stayed in a quaint B & B in Alton, Hampshire, where Jane Austen lived and wrote many of her books. I do not know how to explain it, but I felt I was home in that part of the world. I had no idea about the revelations that were to come in the following days. I left Hampshire and returned to London, where the Sacred Britain Pilgrimage began.

We arrived in Glastonbury, where the veil is so thin that one can slip into another reality and back again before they know what happened. As I walked through the Chalice Well Gardens, I had a remembrance of another lifetime. I was one of the monks at the Glastonbury Abbey. I stood at a distance and watched, as the Abbey burned, helpless to stop it.

In the Garden, where magic abounds, I strolled along the paths, retracing the steps that I had taken ages before. The streams that flow red and white were familiar and welcomed me. The Devic Beings that I had once known were still there, lingering in an adjacent field. They do not live in the realm of linear time; rather, they remain there for eons. The Chalice Well held ancient secrets of an age when the Divine Feminine was in balance with the Divine Masculine. I could have stayed there for days, but the Tor was calling.

The Glastonbury Tor is a high hill, upon which stands a 14th century church tower. The Tor, holds the Arthurian vibration, and is said to be one of the most sacred places in England. The climb up to the top was nearly more than I could handle, but once I reached it, I realized it was all worth it. The hill has its own unique energy that penetrates from deep within. As I stood on the top, overlooking the countryside, pulsating waves passed gently through my Energy Body. More than a legend, Avalon, like Atlantis, still exists in its own time hologram. When one is in Glastonbury, they can momentarily, or for short durations of time, pass through the veil and experience these places. Often, they are believed to be past life memories, rather than simultaneously occurring incarnations.

On the hike back down the Tor, my legs were trembling and my knees began to buckle. It was only due to the kindness and assistance of Vivian, another woman on the pilgrimage, that I could reach the bottom. From a mythical perspective, I thought how symbolic it was that Vivian helped me, considering that a character with the same name was so important in Arthurian lore. I paid the price for that descent for the next year, while my legs healed. I later found out that the magnetic pull on the hill is greater than the Earth's normal magnetic force. I certainly felt it that day.

Stonehenge was impressive of course. The very size of the stones is overwhelming. However, it was Avebury that touched my heart. The energy there, as one languishes among the stones, is very feminine. I noticed, as I basked in the gentle energy of the huge stones, that each one seemed to have a unique vibration. My favorite was the Moon Stone. It is one of the tallest stones at Avebury, standing straight up, as it points to the stars and marks the Summer Solstice.

At the nearby pub, I had one of the best desserts of my life. The Banoffee Pie consisted of a cookie crust, vanilla custard, surrounded with vanilla wafers, and topped with homemade walnut ice cream and hot caramel. It was a work of culinary art.

The next stop was a Crop Circle. The connection with the Star Beings was powerful there. That connection stays with me even today. Most crop circles are found near Ley Lines, electromagnetic conduits for natural Earth energy, allowing the codes, created by the design of the circle, to be transmitted into the Earth's energy grid. In addition, the circles are often found near bodies of water, either above or below the ground. Water has the unique property, like quartz crystal, of retaining the energetic signature, or code, of all that it experiences in its flow, even when that energy is no longer present. The water, which is encoded by the crop circles, flows into streams, rivers, and eventually the ocean, where it vaporizes and returns as rain, ending up in the consumable water supply.

Plants are extremely telepathic. The crops, in the fields where the circles are found, become altered by the energy of the design. Eventually the entire field becomes encoded, as plants communicate through their root system. Before long, other plants for miles are affected. Pollen traveling in the air brings the transformed energy far away from the source. Insects and migrating birds carry the codes even farther, with the pollen that clings to them. In addition, both humans and animals ingest the vibrations, by means of the food products created from the new and improved crops.

Lightworkers that travel to the sites or even view photographs of crop circles also absorb the codes. They are the ones who benefit the most, since they are open to receiving them. When the Internet became the primary source of sharing information, and crop circle photos were available online, the codes began to be distributed exponentially.

As a result of climate change, polar ice caps are melting. Codes that were frozen in past Ice Ages, and which hold the vibration of ancient cultures such as Lemuria and Mu, are now being released into the oceans. The encoded, ancient water is also finding its way to the consumable water supply.

In Cornwall, I stood on the cliff overlooking the wild turquoise sea, with Tintagel Castle resting on top of a high cliff, and Merlin's cave down below. The Arthurian energy enveloped me and once again, the veil between the ancient memories of that time became very thin. Merlin and I go back a long way. I headed straight for the cave, which one can only enter when the tide is low. I had time to commune with Merlin, not the wizard that legend has painted him to be, but the Ascended Master of the Violet Ray. When I viewed the photos, which I took in the cave, there was a Violet Ray in each one of them.

The last stop on the pilgrimage was Roselyn Chapel, in Edinburgh, Scotland. As we crossed over the border from England, to Gretna Green, I thought of the Jane Austen characters that had run off to elope there. As we exited the bus, I heard the strains of Amazing Grace, played on the bagpipes by a man in a kilt. The sound pierced my heart and I nearly doubled over. The recollection of bagpipes playing, as men marched off to war, loomed up from my cellular memory, and I was momentarily consumed in sorrow.

Rosslyn Chapel, in Edinburgh, sits on the Michael Ley Line. It is filled with carvings, containing embedded codes. These codes transcend the Christian aspect of the Chapel and bring one to a much higher place. It was time to go home, but the magic of Sacred Britain forever calls to me to return.

In 2011, I published my third book, Ascension Messages From the Higher Realms - The Process of Conscious Human Evolution. The same year I created my website, ascensionmessages.com. In November, I attended the 11-11-11 Earth-Keeper event in Little Rock, Arkansas. By then, it was clear to me that something energetically significant was happening. The focal point of the previous few years was leading up to 2012. I did not believe, as some others did, it was going to be the end of something, but rather, it was to be the beginning of something new. The following year proved me right.

2012 was the year of the Earth-Keeper Pilgrimage to Sacred Ireland. The magical, Divine Feminine Energy abounds there. Newgrange was mystifying, but the Hill of Tara was where I had left my heart, so long ago. It was a chilly day when we arrived at the Hill, but clear and dry. In fact, on both the pilgrimage to Ireland and the one to England and Scotland, it only rained once. Even the local residents could not believe how good the weather was both those years.

The group stayed on the Hill of Tara for quite some time, but most left and went back to warm up. I was wearing a down jacket, so I was nice and warm, and chose to stay a while longer. Finally, I was the only one left on the Hill. I felt as though I had returned, for I had been there in many lifetimes. Those that had been there with me, in the Golden Age, joined me etherically. I stayed there for as long as I could, basking in the ancient energy, of which I had once been a part. My Heart Chakra merged with the Heart Chakra of the Hill and I felt a completion.

As the bus pulled away, I realized that I had lost one of the new, silver Celtic earrings I had bought in a gift shop at the Cliffs of Moher. I felt sad in a way, because I loved those earrings, but in another way, I was happy that something I held so dear, stayed on the Hill.

It is said that Killarney National Park has the only virgin forest left in Ireland. The Devic Kingdom is alive there. Our wonderfully funny guide, pointed out the huge Faerie rocks covered in moss. We were surely in Magical Ireland.

Skellig Michael was the next stop, but I opted out of it, as I did not want to take the boat ride across the rough sea. Instead, I had a luxurious day on the grounds of the Dunloe Castle Hotel. It began with a delicious, leisurely brunch, with three other women that had also opted out of the boat trip. Afterwards, we walked to the old castle, which is located on the grounds and is surrounded by fantastic gardens and long-standing trees. The other women decided to go by the river to meditate, while I walked into the walled garden to have some privacy.

As I sat on a bench, I noticed there were two Yew trees growing, straight and tall, next to one another. I stepped between them and realized I was in a portal created by their energy. It was a calming, balanced energy, which enticed me to stay for quite some time. When I returned to the hotel, I was informed by the staff that one of the Yew trees was male and called Adam, and the other was female and named Eve.

The New Era

The 12-12-12 Earth-Keeper Star Gate event in Little Rock ushered in the New Era. The energy was indescribable. Everything that Lightworkers had done over the years, culminated at that point to raise the vibration higher than it had ever been, and high enough to allow the Ascension Process to move to the next level. As one of the featured authors, I had a book table in the main conference room, which allowed me to hear all the speakers and feel the magic.

The room was full of individuals whose purpose on this planet was to contribute to the transformation, transmutation, and evolution of the Earth and its inhabitants. We were the ones paving the way for humanity to move into the

Higher Realms. We were the ones holding the Light. It is what we had chosen to do. It was our destiny and it is what mattered to us.

In 2012, Lightworkers became Walking Masters. Going forward, it was up to each of us to hold more Light than ever, and shine it even brighter, so that the entire world will not forget that there still is a Light. I knew then that the Sacred Masculine and Sacred Feminine energies would become balanced and we would be the luminous Light beings we once were. The event was a turning point in the Ascension Process. We were now living in the New Era, a hologramic dimension in tandem with the Third Dimension. Going forward, our purpose was to build the New Era for generations to come.

2014 took me to Sedona with a friend and Soul Sister. We basked in the Energy Vortexes for an entire week. On an earlier trip to Sedona, I had been on a Vortex Tour with Linda Summers, an Earth Angel, who is deeply and psychically attached to the Spirit world of Sedona. On this trip, Linda took my friend and me up a steep, winding road, to the top of Rachel's Knoll.

From there, off in the distance, we could see a cave on the side of a mountain. After leading us in a Soul Activation Meditation, she explained that in a past life in Lemuria, my friend and I came to that cave and planted etheric Lemurian crystals, with the intention that we would find them in this lifetime. That is exactly what happened during the meditation, the energy of the crystals was integrated into both of our energy bodies. It was another quantum leap up the spiral.

The public area of Rachel's Knoll occupies a small spot on top of a steep, high hill. There is a short path, which when followed, ends very close to the edge of a sheer drop to the valley below, with no restraining rail. After the meditation, when I stood up and realized I was several feet from a drop to my death, I wondered how I had not noticed how close I was to the edge. My guides and angels were protecting me and shielding me from fear. Believe me when I say that it was an enlightening experience, but it was the last time I will be going to Rachael's Knoll.

I wrote and published two more books in 2015, Being a Master in the New Era - Integrating the Codes of Ascension, and a novel, SAVING ATLANTIS - A Mystical, Modern Myth. SAVING ATLANTIS was my pride and joy, partly because it brought back memories of my lifetimes in Atlantis.

At the next Earth-Keeper event, I signed up for a session with Sha Na Ra, a crystal skull. The session was to last for twenty minutes. I was joined with two of my Soul Sisters. During the meditation, one of the women told me that the skull asked her to be turned towards me. As she moved the skull in my direction, I placed my hands on the top of it. Almost immediately, a clear vision appeared before me. I was entering the main temple in Atlantis and was being cheered by everyone for writing the book. When one reads Saving Atlantis, they will know why. I was truly honored.

The highlight of the Earth-Keeper Sacred Canada Pilgrimage in 2016, was the trip to Lake Louise, Alberta, in the Canadian Rockies. The turquoise Bow River flows from the glacier-fed lake, through Alberta. Lake Louise, the etheric retreat of Archangel Michael, is one of the most spiritual places I have been.

On the last day of the pilgrimage, while listening to James Tyberonn's meditation, I was transported etherically into the sky above Lake Louise, where I sat in a chair. Archangel Metatron, being more than twelve feet in height, stood right behind me. It was an initiation into my work, going forward, with Archangel Metatron. It all made sense, of course it would be Metatron, as I have enthusiastically embraced Sacred Geometry and Metatron's Cube for years, to prepare for the work ahead.

My Day Job

Since 2003, I have been working as an IT Professional. In 2014, I received a promotion. I am now a Quality Assurance Analyst or in simpler terms, a Software Tester. By becoming more deeply involved in technology, I began to see the importance of the merging of science and spirituality. In essence, it is similar to the balancing of the Divine Masculine and the Divine Feminine.

I have often wondered why, if Conscious Human Evolution is the goal of my Life's Journey, I am working in a corporate environment. When I found myself in that quandary, the Higher Beings stepped in with an explanation. I received a phone call from a woman with whom I had spoken many times on work related calls, which often transitioned into discussions of a personal nature. Once I had sent her one of the books I wrote, hoping it would inspire her. I had not heard from her in years, when unexpectedly, she called to tell me that she did not have long to live. Her life coach guided her to call someone that had inspired her in her life. She said that I was that person. I was truly touched.

Not long after that, I received a text from a woman that had worked in the company but had moved away. A couple of years later, she messaged me to say that I was one of her mentors. As I mentioned the text to a co-worker, she said that I was also one of her mentors. The same day I gave a young woman in the company a Rose Quartz heart and chakra crystal set, because she mentioned that her heart chakra was blocked, and the list goes on. It was clear to me that energy work can be done in the least likely of places, but ones that may be in the most need of healing.

My Way Around

Currently, I am in the process of writing two more books, Balance and Moderation - Achieving the Highest Human State, and a novel, the second of the Saving Atlantis series. I must write or my brain becomes cluttered with ideas. I do not sit around and try to think up things to write, instead the inspiration just comes to me, usually when I am driving, in the shower, or ready to fall asleep. I dictate the main points into my iPhone or iPad, so I do not forget them. I have recently made the decision that when I retire from my corporate job, I will begin a full-time career as an author and literary blogger. It seems the best is yet to come.

After everything I have experienced in my life, I have changed in many ways, but in others, I am still the same. A cheese sandwich is still my favorite food. I continue to love movies. When I am driving, I blast out the same music that I listened to when I was in high school and college, but I also listen to spiritual meditation music.

What have changed are my beliefs, they are now my own, and not necessarily the ones I was taught. Yes, I continue to embrace the standards of morals and decency, which my parents held so high. Some may call my beliefs, out there. I say thank goodness to that! However, I hold fast to what I believe, even if no one else does. Beliefs may change, as one journeys up the infinite spiral of life. What was once true, over time may not be relevant, as one evolves and ascends.

I believe that Star Beings came to this planet for the purpose of seeding humans on the Earth. I am not alone in this belief. There are many indigenous people who have that same belief stored in their cellular memory. They will even tell you from which Star System they originated.

I believe that Archangels, Ascended Masters, and Spiritual Guides are all around me. I speak to them etherically, from my heart, and they answer at once.

I believe that wellness is the default human state and that each person is capable of naturally maintaining a state of well-being.

I also believe that each one of us creates our own reality. This may be difficult to accept, when there is much suffering involved, but no one can know why an individual chose that reality. Perhaps it was decided in a much grander scheme than can be known in the Third Dimension. I may not have chosen the particular events that happened in my life, but I did make choices that positioned me so that they could occur.

I do not believe in thinking of myself as either a victim or a survivor. When one continues to be a victim, they are staying in the vibration of whatever it was that victimized them. The only way forward, is to move on. Everyone that is alive is a survivor and each day should be honored. I do not believe in attaching myself or wearing badges. I prefer to just BE ME.

It is possible to change the past, not by denying that it happened, but by changing one's point of view. Events in one's life can either be viewed as tragic or as a means of learning lessons. When I look back at my life, I see a past that helped create my present situation. I love my life, so all the past events were just stuff along the road that got me here. If one were to ask me about my life, I would have to say that it has been amazing and exciting. Yes, there were painful moments, but there were more that were wonderful. Time does truly heal and only the good memories tend to stand out in the end.

One of the most important things I have learned along the way is to recognize my own power and to set personal boundaries. No matter what anyone else is doing, I must follow my own path and make my own decisions. I listen to my feelings. When I do, my life occurs effortlessly and seamlessly.

We are all observers, watching life as it proceeds. We need not take on the struggle of what is happening in the world. The best we can do is to be kind to those around us and help when we can. First and foremost, we must be kind to ourselves. It is not selfish to do so.

The New Age ushered Lightworkers and Spiritual Seekers into the New Era, as I have dubbed it. An ever so thin gossamer-like veil separates this new dimension from the Third Dimension, allowing one to take part in both realities. The New Era is an etheric, metaphysical place, but very real to those living in it.

The responsibility of those that are aware of their multi-dimensional consciousness is to hold as much Light as possible. Energy work will facilitate keeping one's Light Quotient high, but one must also not immerse themselves into the negative influences of everyday, Third Dimensional goings on. This includes negative influences from media, other people, and one's own thoughts. With practice, it becomes an easy thing to do. I mute the commercials, excuse myself from conversations I do not resonate with, and when I find a negative thought in my mind, I consciously change it to a positive one.

I am so grateful for my life. Yes, there have been dark moments, but, just like this book, the ending is filled with Light. I worked hard to make it so, continuously getting rid of lower vibrating energetic clutter and only keeping the good stuff. I have surrounded myself with beauty and I go through each day gracefully and seamlessly. Yes, I must say, as I journey the infinite spiral of life, all is good, and all is well.

Be Kind

Books by Wendy Ann Zellea

*My Way Around:
  Journeying the Infinite Spiral of Life
*Being a Master in the New Era:
  Integrating the Codes of Ascension
*SAVING ATLANTIS:
  A Mystical, Modern Myth
*Ascension Messages from the Higher Realms:
  The Process of Conscious Human Evolution
*Do You Want to Be Happy NOW?:
  2nd Edition
*Life is Good, All is Well:
  Everything is Vibration

Available on Amazon

About the Author

Wendy Ann Zellea is an Ascension Messenger and Luminary.

She is the author of 6 metaphysical books and numerous inspirational articles. She presents esoteric concepts in a clear writing style for a wide audience.

Wendy has been a college English instructor, musician, singer and composer, and IT Professional.

Her work focuses upon bringing through information, from the Higher Realms, for living in the New Era.

AscensionMessages.com
AnEnlightenedAuthor.com

Made in the USA
Middletown, DE
29 October 2020